SOUTHAMPTON AND D-DAY

Published by

**Oral History
City Heritage
Southampton City Council
Civic Centre, Southampton, SO14 7LP**

Written, compiled and edited by

Ingrid Peckham

Oral History compiled and edited by

Donald Hyslop and Sheila Jemima

Photography by

John Lawrence

© Southampton City Council
ISBN 1 872649 04 1
1994

Design by
Graphics Services, Directorate of Community Services, Southampton City Council.

Produced by
Oral History, City Heritage, Southampton City Council.

Printed by Printarea Limited, Units 4&5 Newgate Lane, Fareham, Hants, PO14 1BP.

Front cover: Rockleigh Road in mid 1944, taken from the house on the corner of Hill Lane and Rockleigh Road, Southampton. (Bert Bagg)

CONTENTS

Introduction	1
Background	3
Early Preparations For The Invasion of Northern Europe	5
Final Preparations	19
D-Day - 6th June 1944	32
After D-Day	36
American and British Troops About Town	65
War Brides	75
Sources	76

ACKNOWLEDGMENTS

We wish to thank the following people for their assistance during the research for this book. Rachel Wragg and Alastair Arnott of the City Heritage Collections Management Team, for their help with the photographic and other collections at Melbourne Street. Sue Woolgar, the City Archivist, and Andrew George and Mark Baverstock, the staff at the Southampton Record Office, for retrieving numerous archives from the depths of the Civic Centre. Also Peter Ashton at the Southern Daily Echo library, the Special Collections staff at the University of Southampton, and the Department of Photographs staff at the Imperial War Museum.

In particular, this book would not have been produced without the hard work of the following people, who are especially to be thanked. Gaylene Lueger for typing up the script and dealing with the numerous edits. John Lawrence, the City Arts Photographer, for printing off the mass of photographs. Barry Taylor, Diane Brindle, Sandra Barnett and Wendy Barker at Graphics Services, for laying out the Operation Overload text.

We thank the following organisations for allowing us to reproduce material:-

The Trustees of the Imperial War Museum, London
Southern Daily Echo
Royal Corps of Transport Museum, Aldershot
National Archives of Canada
Southampton Record Office
St. Johns First School, Southampton

Building caissons for the Mulberry Harbours in the Old Docks, Southampton, 1944. (ABP)

INTRODUCTION

This book is about the role of Southampton and its people in the long build-up to D-Day and the months that followed. It is also about the impact on life in the town of the presence of thousands of troops, particularly Americans, in the last years of the Second World War

Operation Overlord, launched on D-Day 6th June 1944, was the largest military invasion in history. It was the beginning of the liberation of Northern Europe from fascism. 156,000 Allied troops landed on the Normandy beaches on D-Day alone. 10,000 men were killed or wounded on the first day. 2,000 Americans lost their lives taking Omaha Beach, where the heaviest fighting took place.

The people of Southampton welcomed the invasion, being weary after 4^1/$_2$ years of war, but many had relatives and friends taking part in the landings.

Local people played an important part in the preparations and follow-up activities. Factory workers produced munitions and landing craft. Shipyard workers repaired, refitted or built many of the vessels used. Dockworkers in the port loaded and unloaded military equipment.

Many local people helped build the Mulberry Harbours. Others provided medical care, and cooked food for the troops passing through the town. Members of the American Army 14th Major Port were based in Southampton for over three years. 3^1/$_2$ million British, American, Canadian and other troops passed through the town on their way to France. Later the town was used as a leave centre by troops. This book is a tribute to all those people who lived and worked in the town or passed through on their way to the battlefields of Europe.

SOURCES

Most of the photographs in this book come from two collections of hitherto largely unpublished photographs, now held by Southampton City Heritage.

The first of these is the Associated British Port (ABP) collection, consisting of photographs taken by Southern Railway, which ran the port during the Second World War.

The second collection is that of Captain Dalton Newfield who was Provost Marshal of the 14th Port. This mainly contains pictures of American service personnel both on and off duty.

The bias towards pictures of Americans in the book reflects the contents of these two collections, which in turn reflects the sheer scale of the American activities in the port, particularly in the months after D-Day. By contrast, far fewer photographs were taken during the few weeks up to D-Day itself, when the British and Canadian assault forces were in the town and tight security restrictions were in place. Some photographs of British troops from the Imperial War Museum archive have been used to complete the overall picture.

Many extracts from the diaries of Arthur Daniel Cox have been used. Daniel Cox was a joiner and charge hand with Beazley's, a local ship repair firm. He was 36 year when war was declared in September 1939. He then lived in Oakbank Road, Woolston with his wife Elsie, his 11 year old son Ted and his mother. The family were bombed out in September 1940, and eventually moved to Carisbrooke Drive, Bitterne. In April 1941, they took a room in Hedge End, where they slept during the heavy air raids. Daniel Cox kept a diary throughout the war.

The memories of Oral History interviewees and correspondents are also included. There is a full list of their names at the back of the book.

A full list of photographic and other sources is given at the back of the book.

The Wedding of Daniel and Elsie Cox in 1926. (Cox Collection)

Three-piece landing craft being fitted together in the docks, 1942/43. (ABP)

BACKGROUND

For Southampton, the spring of 1942 was a turning point in the Second World War. In February of that year, Lease-Lend cargoes began to arrive in the port from America. Then followed the gradual build-up to D-Day and Operation Overlord.

The port had been closed to ocean-going ships in the summer of 1940, after Dunkirk and the fall of France to the Germans. The English Channel became too dangerous for large ships, and the threat of invasion by Germany meant that Southampton was a front-line target. Registered dock workers were sent to work in other local industries and the docks were used only by small coastal craft.

The summer of 1940 saw the start of the heavy air raids on the town, which continued well into 1941. The worst raids, Southampton's Blitz, occurred on November 23rd, November 30th and December 1st, 1940. Although air raids continued throughout the war, they were never again as bad as on those nights.

Above Bar Street, looking north from the Bargate, in the mid 1940's. (City Heritage Collections)

By the end of 1941, the threat of invasion by Germany, although still present, had lessened, and the U-boats were sinking fewer ships. The United States of America had joined the war and was sending aid in the form of Lease-Lend cargoes to Britain.

On 6th February 1942, Southampton Docks were reopened to receive the first of the Lease-Lend cargoes to arrive in the port. After that, the Docks remained open to ocean-going ships.

MONDAY 2nd FEBRUARY 1942 *"...Most of the men in the yard have got hold of a story about the docks being reopened for cargo work. Four ships are supposed to arrive today. Whether this is true or not, I cannot find out from official sources." (**Cox**)*

The registered dock workers were recalled to the port industry. The arrival of each ship was secret, and it was not possible to give good notice of when the dock workers were needed. This caused problems for the employers who had to release the dock workers. The Borough Council's Electricity Department complained that, with the shortage of labour, it could not afford to lose the dock workers, who had been retrained to work in the town's Electricity Undertaking. Other council departments also protested.

Work in the port continued day and night. The volume of traffic in 1942 and 1943 approximated that of pre-war years. The cargoes came mainly from the USA and Canada and included food, timber, metals and military equipment.

The local shipyards were busy throughout the war, repairing and converting ships. Over 10,000 ships passed through these yards during the war. Thornycroft and Co. built many new ships at their Woolston yard. Other local industries changed over to the production of military goods.

Barrels of Lease-Lend fruit juice in Shed 32, Old Docks, 7th February 1942. (ABP)

Lease-Lend cargoes being offloaded, 7th February 1942. (ABP)

Lease-Lend cargoes being packed into rail trucks (note the dock equipment), 16th February 1942. (ABP)

EARLY PREPARATIONS FOR THE INVASION OF NORTHERN EUROPE

In the autumn of 1940, the War Office carried out a preliminary survey of the Southampton area, with a view to using it as a base for the invasion of Northern Europe.

In April 1942, the British and American governments agreed to start the build-up for this invasion. A survey was made of the port. In July 1942, Combined Operations Military Movement Control set up headquarters in the South Western Hotel. The Royal Navy Flag Officer also set up headquarters there. The Southampton area, extending from near Romsey in the west, to Hedge End in the east and Bushfield Camp near Winchester in the north, was designated Area "C".

Further plans for the invasion were agreed in early 1943. The date for the landings was set for May 1944 but this was later moved back to June 1944. The invasion was to be known as Operation Overlord.

Landing craft and other vessels were arriving in the docks in 1942. The docks authority and Royal Navy Flag Officer allocated berths for the craft in the Old and New Docks. Local shipyards began to do repair and refitting work on these craft.

Meanwhile, troops passed through the port for military exercises and operations. One of the latter was the Dieppe raid of August 1942, when 10,000 Canadian and British troops attempted to capture the port of Dieppe for a few days, to test the strength of the German defences. The raid failed badly but the lessons learnt were used in the planning of Operation Overlord.

WEDNESDAY 22nd APRIL 1942 *"...Worked until seven on lifeboats. Five barges came to the yard yesterday and work on them commenced today. The job being run by W.P. I understand these barges are for invasion purposes, and that Campers, Thorny's and Whites are doing similar work.... Tonights news gave an account of another raid by troops on France. Not much detail yet. The troops were ashore for about two hours."* ***(Cox)***

WEDNESDAY 20th MAY 1942 *"...Rumours in the yard today that after this week the port is to be closed for cargo traffic and the docks are to be taken over by the Admiralty and military, in readiness for the invasion of the continent. How true this is, time will tell. I believe that barges are already being loaded in the docks..."****(Cox)***

WEDNESDAY 15th JULY 1942 *"...Started work on Harlands job today on booby hatches. The barges have become a rush. There are about 180 to do. Worked as usual until seven....The war news from Russia just as serious."* ***(Cox)***

TUESDAY 18th AUGUST 1942 *"...Some of the men working in the docks said that there has been great activity all day, many troops arriving and the lorry drivers said that traffic has been very heavy in the town, military and civil police being on duty at many points. There was a warning after nine this morning and the "danger" signal blew. Shortly after there was a lot of gunfire in the South, which continued for some time. No actual activity here. A second short warning later and two more this evening."* ***(Cox)***

WEDNESDAY 19th AUGUST 1942 *"...A day of excitement and alarms. At seven o'clock this morning it was given out on the news that British troops had landed in the Dieppe area, and fierce fighting was taking place. At one o'clock reports that tanks had been landed and that air activity was terrific. The last statement was "operations continuing". Work went along until round about half past three, when the sirens sounded. The "danger" went on a few minutes later, and gunfire was heard in the S and S.W. This went on for some time, guns firing all round, but not in the vicinity. Suddenly a plane came in from the East and all the local guns opened up. A very heavy cannonade for a while. Guns were still firing in the distance and it was well after four before the "All Clear" sounded. At quarter past five another warning and from that time until half past seven there was an almost continuous rumble of gunfire in the S and S.W. The "All Clear" went at 7.45. The six o'clock news did not give many more details of the British landing, and I was anxious to hear the nine o'clock bulletin but when* it came on I was disappointed. Our troops had re-embarked after being ashore for nine hours. We had lost 95 planes against 89 German. We had destroyed a gun nest, an ammunition dump and a radiolocation station. Casualties heavy on both sides. A full report would be issued later..." *(Cox)*

THURSDAY 27th AUGUST 1942 "...Worked until seven o'clock on some jobs but the men seem lazy and listless and the job goes along very slowly. Eight men coming back to the yard tomorrow but on the new M.T. Boat. Most of the barges in the inner dock are finished and until the authorities decide where and when the next batch will be moored nothing much can be done..." *(Cox)*

Army exercise - loading and unloading vehicles in the New Docks, 11th November 1942 . (ABP)

MONDAY 16th NOVEMBER 1942 "... Joe...told me that two commando ships left the docks this afternoon, fully loaded. But I expect their mission is secret, and unless anything unforeseen happens, we will hear nothing about it. ..."*(Cox)*

WEDNESDAY 3rd FEBRUARY 1943 "...For a wonder, went to a social and dance this evening with Elsie and Doris, held at the Gymnasium of St Marys' College and run by Beazleys' Home Guard. We arrived about half past seven and stopped until eleven. It was not too bad, but the only objection was there was too much dance and not enough social. But if they run any more perhaps this will be remedied. It was nearly midnight before we went to bed. Todays news is that the fighting at Stalingrad is at last ended, the remaining Germans having been either killed or captured. So ends one of the most decisive battles of the war. At the moment, Stalingrad is nearly 200 miles behind the fighting line and it seems only a short time ago that the fall of the City seemed inevitable. Two warnings today, one this evening having the "danger" in operation. There was some gunfire and we could see the shell bursts, but it did not last very long." *(Cox)*

WEDNESDAY 5th MAY 1943 "...Worked until five o'clock on some odd jobs. As I was coming home there was a long convoy of mechanised troops passing through to town. Some of the lorries had light machine guns mounted on the front and there was a man on each, with finger on trigger. Several people living outside the town have told me of much troop movement these last few days..." *(Cox)*

THURSDAY 13th MAY 1943 "...Todays main news is that organised resistance in North Africa is now ended. Von Amin is captured, with most of his staff. Fantastic scenes were witnessed when thousands of prisoners gave themselves up. Very few managed to get away. On Sunday, the Church bells are to ring and special services of thanksgiving are to be held. ..."*(Cox)*

New facilities had to be built in the docks, and railway sidings were extended.

"Special loading facilities had also to be provided in the way of 'hards' for the vast majority of the ships that were to compose the grand armada. Designed

to enable them to discharge their loads direct on to an open beach, the bows of the tank landing craft (L.C.T.) and tank landing ships (L.S.T.) took the form of collapsible ramps. For loading purposes it accordingly became necessary to construct a series of 'hards'. Increased slip, grid and mooring accommodation was also a pressing necessity, as was the provision of a score of other facilities." **(Knowles)**

Hards S1, S2 and S3 were completed in February 1943. Hard S4 at Northam was completed in February 1944. Building rubble from bomb damaged sites nearby was used to build these hards.

Small boat being unloaded from a train at 101 Berth, New Docks, 7th May 1943. (ABP)

Landing craft built at the Southern Railway Works, Eastleigh, arriving in the Old Docks, 29th April 1943. (ABP)

Landing craft built at Southern Railway Works, Eastleigh, arriving in the New Docks, 12th May 1943. (ABP)

Tank landing craft arriving in the Docks in three sections, were lifted by 50 ton crane and joined together at Southampton. (ABP)

Landing craft being painted by dock workers. (ABP)

Americans Arrive in the Port

The US Army 14th Major Port Transportation Corps arrived in Southampton in July 1943. Initially their headquarters were in the Maritime Chambers in the Old Docks, but they later moved to the Civic Centre. The Borough Council granted the use of "certain rooms and part of the basement" of the Civic Centre, free of charge. The 14th Port also had a headquarters on Hoglands Park. The first Port Commander in Southampton was Major Warren D. Lamport, later replaced by Col. Walter D. McCord. In May 1944, Lt. Col. Leo J. Meyer took over. In July 1944 he in turn was replaced by Col. Sherman L. Kiser.

The main role of the 14th Port in Operation Overlord was to coordinate the shipment of American troops, military equipment and stores through the port. They worked with representatives from Southern Railway, the unions, local traders, Government ministers and the British Army and Navy, on port committees.

After D-Day, the 14th Port landed incoming wounded and German prisoners of war. They were also responsible for vessel salvage and investigating accident liability. There was a 14th Port Provost Corps, responsible for policing American troops about the town. After the war, the 14th Port repatriated American soldiers and embarked British war brides for the USA and Canada. The 14th Port stayed in Southampton until November 1946.

In the spring of 1944, battalions attached to the 14th Port arrived in the town. Among these were the 499th Port Battalion, which arrived in February 1944, bringing mobile dock equipment. In May 1944, stevedores from the 552nd Port Company arrived. This company is recorded in the 14th Port Books (City Heritage Collections) as being composed of about 200 "coloured" soldiers with white officers. The 14th Port, like the American armed forces as a whole at the time, was segregated. The 14th Port Books state that black soldiers were in segregated units, with separate work details, billets, recreational facilities and Red Cross clubs.

Officers of the 14th Port were billeted in the Polygon Hotel. Enlisted men were initially billeted in Ascupart Road School and later in the Blighmont Barracks off Millbrook Road and in camps outside the town, including one in Ashurst.

In March 1944, American civilian tug crews, employed by the 14th Port, arrived and were quartered in the dock area. They were to operate some of the tugs used to tow the Mulberry Harbour sections to France.

On 1st May 1944 the US Naval Advanced Amphibious Base arrived in Southampton, setting up headquarters at the Star Hotel. They remained in Southampton until July 1945, providing logistic support for US naval forces in the area, in cooperation with the Royal Navy. They were initially commanded by Lt. Commander Richard S. Aldrich, USNR, and later by Lt. Commander Hamilton Moses, USNR.

About 50 members of the American Women's Army Auxiliary Corps were accommodated at Highfield Hall by the University College, before leaving for France.

"Significant changes in the activities at Southampton Docks during the latter part of 1943 presaged the nearness of big events. A Port Headquarters for the U.S. Army was established at the Docks, while increasing quantities of military stores and equipment, including guns, tanks, and vehicles of all descriptions arrived in the ships bringing Lease-Lend materials from the U.S.A." **(Southampton Docks Handbook, 1947)**

Local Anticipation in 1943

The prevailing government and military view was that the scale of operations and the build-up of troops and equipment required, would not allow the invasion of Northern Europe to take place before the Spring of 1944. Many people however, had felt frustrated since 1940, by the failure to start this "Second Front".

In 1943 there was much speculation about the imminence of the invasion. In June 1943, the Southern Evening Echo headline read "Amphibious Operations on a large scale predicted by Churchill". Another article the same month spoke of mock invasion exercises for the forthcoming "invasion of Europe". The increased military activity in the docks fuelled local anticipation. In July 1943 the secret HARLEQUIN exercise took place, which determined the port's capacity for troops and equipment for the invasion.

The Star Hotel, US Navy Headquarters.
(Newfield)

Tanks in transit on the Southern Railway,
July 1943. (ABP)

The "Alcoa Scout" discharging American
locomotives, 5th July 1943. (ABP)

American tanks being unloaded from the ship
"John Chandler" by 50 ton crane in No 7 Dry
Dock, 16th August 1943. (ABP)

Map reproduction trailer being discharged from
the ship "Stephen C. Foster",
11th November 1943. (ABP)

General view of the main pier at Marchwood
whilst under construction in 1943.
(RCT Museum)

When the invasion did not happen in 1943, there was disappointment in some quarters.

FRIDAY 30th JULY 1943 *"...Heard today from several sources that guns and tanks are being loaded on to ships and barges in the docks. We have received a rush job of Notice boards for the Sea Transport, to be used for embarkation purposes, so perhaps things are moving again..."* ***(Cox)***

A letter from the Chief Constable, dated 6th August 1943, concerning Defence Regulation 13A:-

"In connection with a Military Exercise to be arranged shortly, I am requested by the Military Authorities to forward you the enclosed Direction No. 1 by the G.O.C. in C., Southern Command, and Warning Notice, bringing into force a number of restrictions.

You will observe in para. 3 of the Warning Notice that the restrictions will be relaxed or suspended in considerable portions of the area. In Southampton the areas will be affected intermittently during the Exercise will be:-

(a) Hill Lane, north of Bellemoor Inn.
(b) Bassett Wood Road; Bassett Green Road (between Chilworth Cross Roads and Bassett Wood Road).
(c) Furzedown Road.
(d) Certain streets in the vicinity of the Royal Pier, Southampton.
(e) Certain streets in the south part of Woolston.

The Police are giving the necessary advice to residents in each locality who are affected by the restrictions, and I enclose specimens of special permits which are being issued in all appropriate cases. The restrictions begin on 17th August.

Although reference is made in para.2(e) of the Warning Notice to the possibility of a curfew, I am informed that a curfew is unlikely to be imposed during the Exercise.

The only publicity being given to the Exercise is by the posting of Direction No. 1 and the Warning Notice at police stations, railway stations and post offices.

I shall be glad if you will exhibit the Warning Notice for the information of your staff." **(SRO SC/TC File 195/21)**

SUNDAY 8th AUGUST 1943 *"...Heard this morning the Southampton area (extending to Romsey, Winchester, Horndean and Fareham in the East) will be a restricted district from August 17th. I have not seen the notices. Various rumours circulating as usual. A curfew is to be imposed at once, we will be heavily bombed again and such like stories. The bombing part unfortunately, is more likely to be true, for it is fairly evident that Southampton will be an important port when the invasion of Europe does take place."* ***(Cox)***

TUESDAY 24th AUGUST 1943 *"...Worked as usual until seven o'clock. Did not feel very cheerful. B.K. has been telling me various things he has heard officially from H.G. headquarters. Heavy bombing raids are expected on the town, with a possibility of airborne troops being landed. If and when we attempt a landing on the Continent. I know that the Anti-aircraft defenses have been strengthened during the last week or two and there are reports that the fire services have been augmented from other towns. Although this might be a lot of hooey, yet the signs are that something big is pending, and I can't look to the future with any pleasurable anticipation. Last night we raided Berlin and lost fifty eight bombers in the process. The Quebec talks have ended and the other news is that Himmler has been appointed Minister of the Interior in Germany."* ***(Cox)***

WEDNESDAY 25th AUGUST 1943 *"...Worked until seven o'clock. Heard that by the end of next week all the big boats in the docks must leave. Whether this is true or not remains to be seen. Our vessel must be finished by Tuesday..."* ***(Cox)***

One of the largest "A1" caissons being completed in the Old Docks, 1944. (ABP)

Bombardons under construction in No. 7 Dry Dock, 1944. (ABP)

Large caissons being completed, 1944. (ABP)

Sections of Whale floating roadways being assembled at Marchwood, 1943/44. (RCT Aldershot)

One of the smaller "B2" caissons being moved by tugs, 1944. (ABP)

Whale pontoons, with their "spuds", being assembled near No. 7 Dry Dock. Rhino pontoons in the foreground, 1944. (ABP)

Whale pontoons, with their upright "spuds", being assembled near No. 7 Dry Dock. Rhino pontoons are being put together in the foreground, 1944. (ABP)

Rhino pontoons being assembled near No. 7 Dry Dock. A Whale pontoon is being tested in the background, 1944. (ABP)

FRIDAY 10th DECEMBER 1943 *"...Spent the day as usual at work. The building job where the chaps from the yard have to go now turns out to be Lepe, and not Portsmouth."* **(Cox)**

FRIDAY 31st DECEMBER 1943 *"Fine most of the day, although cloudy at times, and once or twice a damp of rain. Cold this morning, becoming warmer during the afternoon. A slight rain early this evening, clear and fine later. Worked all day on some jobs. Spent the evening reading. Tonights news is that Russians have recaptured Zhitomir. Did not stop up to see the new year in, but went to bed at quarter past eleven. As usual, most people are talking of "Victory in 1944" but I have heard that cry every year since the war started. Certainly things at the moment are in our favour, but look how long our Italian campaign has taken."* **(Cox)**

Car drivers in the port, March 1944. (ABP)

Bells Ring in 1944 at Southampton

For the first time since 1939 church bells rang out the dying year and ushered in the new in Southampton. And outside the ruins of Holy Rood Church there was the biggest New Year's Eve crowd seen there since the war to observe the old custom of "dancing on the asphalt".

The bells of Holy Rood crashed to the bottom of the tower when the church was burnt out during a raid, but the band of bell-ringers, determined to keep tradition alive, obtained a concession to ring the bells of near-by St. Michael's. And so once more Sotonians heard the peal sound the knell of 1943 and ring in joyously the year of high hopes. .....

On the Asphalt

For the dancing on the asphalt the programme was arranged by A.R.P. wardens. During the past two years the gatherings have not been large but the custom had been kept alive by the wardens, even at the height of the heavy air raids on the town. In 1940 the tradition of ringing out the Old Year and ringing in the New Year was kept by striking the midnight hour on a large frying-pan! Last night soldiers joined in the celebrations. As is usual, popular songs were sung, and the gathering dispersed following the National Anthem.

Dancers' Night

Thousands of Sotonians danced their way into 1944. Not only were the down-town halls packed to capacity, but in the suburbs almost every available building had been booked for a New Year's Eve dance. In hotels where dinner-dances were held revellers linked arms and sang Auld Lang Syne, and drank toasts to 1944 at midnight.

(Echo, 1st January 1944)

FINAL PREPARATIONS

In early 1944, the Southampton Co-ordinating Committee was making secret plans connected with D-Day. The committee comprised representatives from government ministries, the local authority, police, port authorities and the military. The committee devised plans aimed at ensuring the movement of military convoys in all circumstances, including air raids and gas attacks. It was expected that the Germans would mount large-scale air raids on Southampton once D-Day had begun, if not before, and nothing was to hinder the success of the military operation. In the event, many of these plans proved to be unnecessary as the air raids did not happen.

One hundred and twenty military vehicles per hour would be on the roads. At a meeting on 14th March 1944 it was stated that:

"Movement will be in small closed up columns, of some 14 vehicles each, more or less continuously round the clock for a period of some weeks. There will be short intervals between these small columns into which all priority traffic will be able to be fitted and probably most of the normal traffic as well. There will be larger columns of up to 40 vehicles at infrequent intervals, but notice of the movement of these should be available. ...naval movement would be largely by single vehicles at various times, totalling about 100 a day. Some of these would be high priority, others not." **(SRO SC/TC Files 194/9)**

Military traffic was to have absolute priority. Some civilian traffic had higher priority than others, for instance transport for essential workers. Traffic management plans included "no overtaking" signs on some roads and the suspension of certain tram stops. The public utilities were to notify the highway authority before doing roadworks.

Arrangements were made to provide materials, equipment and civilian and military labour to repair bomb-damaged roads, bridges and hards. Gas decontamination squads were organised.

In the event of heavy air raids, the local population was supposed to "Stand Firm" so that refugees did not block the roads. But experience in the Blitz of 1940/41 suggested that the numbers of refugees or "trekkers" would not be great enough to cause problems for the military convoys. Plans were made to evacuate the school children still in the town, as well as mothers with children of school age and under, once a raid had started, but not before. Preparations were made for the arrival of wounded Allied and German troops and civilian casualties.

More static water tanks were built in early 1944 to increase the water supply in case of large scale fires. The question of water priority between the National Fire Service and the military was said to be "prickly", but the military had priority. The Mayor issued an appeal in the local press asking people to save water.

"Of course Woolston was so badly bombed at the bottom end down Bridge Road, all the houses were so bad that they used all that area for training the D-Day troops for the house-to-house fighting because it was a lot of ruins anyway so they just carried on using it as ruins!" **(Bramwell Taylor)**

It became more and more difficult to find space in the port for the various projects. In addition to the Mulberry construction project and the storage of landing craft, the port had to handle the troops and equipment arriving in the port, and the Lease-Lend cargoes.

Blitz sites were levelled to provide parking space for military vehicles. A piece of Corporation property in the New Docks, between Dock Gates 8 and 9, was requisitioned in January 1944. (This land was used as a POW camp after D-Day).

Buildings from private houses to commercial premises were requisitioned, as were all the schools. The schools were turned into barracks, first aid and medical centres and mortuaries. Taunton's School became a POW camp. A shed on Town Quay became a barracks. The Central Baths and Old Town Mortuary were allocated for use as mortuaries. The Royal Victoria Hospital at Netley was given over to the Americans. Other local hospitals were cleared and admissions restricted shortly before D-Day.

Berths 105 and 106 in the New Docks and Berth

49 in the Old Docks were used to moor landing craft. Then in April 1944, more landing craft arrived from Portland and had to be berthed.

SATURDAY 11th MARCH 1944 *"...These last few days have been remarkable for the amount of military traffic on the roads. Troops, guns, tanks and vehicles of every description have been going to, and coming from Southampton. One can't see sense or reason for it all, but I suppose it is all part of a plan. But I still do not anticipate an invasion of Europe yet." (Cox)*

FRIDAY 14th APRIL 1944 *"...Worked until five. The shop dead again. Spent the evening in the shed. At half past one this morning was awakened by the sirens. I got up and went outside. There was no air activity, but there must have been a huge convoy on the move in Bitterne Road, for the noise of the tanks was shattering. Judging by the clatter and banging, some of the stuff was very big. The lights of the convoy made a soft glow in the sky. The "All Clear" went in five and twenty minutes and long after I had returned to bed I could hear the rumble of the traffic and it was a long time before I slept. At work, one of the chaps said he heard the noise at Chandlers Ford, where he lives, and he thought the convoy was at Swaythling." (Cox)*

Restrictions on population movement

On 31st March 1944, Regulated Area (No. 2) Order was issued, establishing a 10 mile wide coastal strip of land from the Wash to Lands End, in which the movement of people was restricted. The area was closed to all visitors. Guards were placed at railway stations, bus depots and on roads entering the zone. Only residents could travel to the Isle of Wight. Nobody was allowed to enter or leave Southampton without a permit - armed guards manned road barriers. Direction No. 26 was issued under the Regulated Area (No. 2) Order, to come into force on 19th April 1944. Direction No. 20 was issued under the same order. These Directions placed further restrictions on local people. Direction No.26 applied to parts of Britannia Road and Belvidere Road, Northam. It remained in force until June 14th 1944. It delineated the affected area as follows:-

"In the COUNTY OF SOUTHAMPTON in the COUNTY BOROUGH of SOUTHAMPTON: An area lying within a line drawn from a point on the foreshore of the RIVER ITCHEN where the building of Messrs SUMMERS & PAYNE joins CORNICKS GARAGE and thence WESTWARDS across BELVIDERE ROAD to include the dwelling houses at the SOUTHERN end of BRITANNIA ROAD thence following the WEST side of BELVIDERE ROAD excluding all premises adjacent thereto SOUTHWARDS to a point opposite the NORTH boundary of Messrs HOOPER & ASHLEYS yard and then EAST to the foreshore." (SRO SC/TC File 195/21)

Direction No. 20, applying to the Weston Esplanade - High Street - Platform Road area, remained in force until July 4th 1944.

Preparations were shielded from aerial view by smoke screens and camouflage.

FABIUS

The military exercise FABIUS, which was a full scale rehearsal for D-Day itself, took place in early May 1944. It involved the briefing and movement of troops and equipment from the marshalling camps to the docks, embarkation and then a mock landing on Hayling Island. As the first wave of 3,000 British troops left the camps, they were replaced by the second wave and so on, ending with the first wave of Americans. Military Movement Control and the 14th Port worked together in co-ordinating the exercise. FABIUS was completed in mid-May, the troops being returned to their original camps. Before FABIUS began, the camps were enclosed behind fences of barbed wire and were closely guarded.

"...certain camps embraced residences housing civilian occupants, which meant giving them the choice of evacuating the camp or becoming bound by military security measures." (Knowles)

On 24th May, 1944 the camps were sealed and the British assault forces fully briefed. Final loading began on 31st May 1944 and was completed 4th June 1944.

WARNING NOTICE

1. NOTICE IS HEREBY GIVEN that within the area(s) specified in Direction No. 26 by the General Officer Commanding-in-Chief, Southern Command, a number of restrictions will come into effect from the date stated in the Direction and continue until further notice.

2. The general effect of these restrictions is as follows :—
   - (a) Nobody, except a resident holding a Certificate of Residence, will be allowed to enter the area(s) without a Special Permit or Temporary Pass which will only be granted for urgent business reasons or for some other purpose as specified in paragraph 4 below, (but see paragraphs 3 and 7).
   - (b) Both vehicles and pedestrians will be obliged to follow the directions of the civil Police and members of His Majesty's and Allied Forces on duty, and may be prohibited altogether from using certain roads at certain times.
   - (c) The carrying of cameras, telescopes and binoculars on any highway or in any public place without a Permit will be forbidden. The use of cameras is also subject to the Control of Photography Orders. (See paragraph 6 (b) below).

3. All persons, except residents, desiring to visit or remain in the area(s) should therefore apply in writing to the police station nearest to the place where they intend to visit or remain in, for the information whether a Special Permit or Temporary Pass is required. All applications must show the purpose of the visit, the place or person to be visited, the duration of the visit and the number of the applicant's National Registration Identity Card. No application need be made by residents for Certificates of Residence, which will be distributed by the police.

Hotel and Boarding Housekeepers and private residents in the area(s) who are expecting visitors to stay should warn them that they will not be permitted to enter the area(s) until further notice except for an "approved purpose."

4. The following reasons for visiting the area(s) will normally be regarded as an "approved purpose" but each application will be considered on its merits and there is no guarantee that these reasons will be accepted in all cases. The decision of the Chief Constable, or of the Military Authorities, to grant or refuse a Permit or Pass in any case will be final, and no explanation of an adverse decision can be given.
   - (a) Essential visits on business connected with the person's employment or occupation (i.e., visits which are not of a routine nature and cannot be postponed).
   - (b) Visits to near relatives who are seriously ill.

   NOTE: The term "near relative" means a member of one's own immediate family (including grand-parents and uncles and aunts, but NOT cousins).

5. Details of these restrictions are given in the Direction by the General Officer Commanding-in-Chief, Southern Command, copies of which are exhibited in the area(s). Regulated Area Bye-Laws (No. 2) 1944 will also apply. Other Orders involved are the Control of Photography Orders (No. 1) 1939 and (No. 5) 1942, and the Protected Areas Orders (Nos. 10, 11, and 12) 1944.

6.
   - (a) Applications for Permits to carry cameras, telescopes or binoculars should be addressed in writing to the nearest police station.
   - (b) No permits to carry cameras, telescopes or binoculars are required by any constable, any member of the Armed Forces of the Crown or of an Allied Force, the Women's Royal Naval Service, Queen Alexandra's Royal Naval Nursing Service, the Royal Observer Corps, any master or member of the crew of a ship or vessel, any employee of the Corporation of Trinity House or of the Commissioners of the Northern Lighthouses, any pilot holding a licence issued in virtue of the Pilotage Act 1913, any member of any Lifeboat Service, the National Fire Service, the Civil Defence Services, any raid spotter, or any employee of the National Buildings Record Council, while acting in the course of their duty as such.

7. The following forms or Special Identity Documents will be recognised in lieu of Special Permits provided only that the Holders are on duty :—
   DR Form 1, DR Form 12, DR Form 20, NR 107, NR 107A, Police Warrant Card, Military, Naval and R.A.F. or Allied Forces Identity Documents.

8. PERSONS WHO CONTRAVENE THE DIRECTIONS BYE-LAWS AND ORDERS REFERRED TO IN PARAGRAPH 5 ARE LIABLE TO PROSECUTION AND ON CONVICTION BY A COURT OF SUMMARY JURISDICTION TO A PENALTY OF THREE MONTHS IMPRISONMENT OR A FINE OF £100 OR BOTH.

S.C.P. 118 4/44 5,000 S.P. 96358

Warning Notice with Direction No. 26. (SRO SC/TC File 195/21)

SATURDAY 22nd APRIL 1944 *"...Southampton is packed with troops. There are camps on every available piece of spare ground. Anti-aircraft guns and searchlights are being placed in various new places in and around the town. Invasion fever is gripping everyone, but somehow I don't think anything will happen just yet." **(Cox)***

TUESDAY 25th APRIL 1944 *"...Two landing barges which we are fitting out are now wanted in a hurry. The 30th of this month is named for the completion of several jobs." **(Cox)***

SUNDAY 30th APRIL 1944 *"...Had a rush job come in, 174 notice boards. Was out in the shed this evening, but I can't get any luck with my polishing. No matter what I do I don't seem to be able to fill the grain of the wood, and the polish comes up rough. But I must keep on until I find the secret. Still the same lack of news from any of the war fronts, but all day long there has been great activity in the air, many bunches of planes passing over. And it has been the same after dark this evening. At midnight the sirens sounded. I did not get up, and the "All Clear" went shortly afterwards." **(Cox)***

MONDAY 1st MAY 1944 *"...Worked until seven o'clock. Started work on 20 ladders, which seem to be for scaling purposes. The strings are of pitch pine, 4 1/2" x 1 1/2", and a devil of a job we have had sawing them from 8" x 8" bulks. Did some more in the shed on arrival home, but was just as unsuccessful polishing. This morning just before six o'clock, planes began to pass over, and for over an hour there was one continuous drone. The sky was a bit overcast, so could not see what was going on. Many people thought the invasion had started. All day long, squadrons of planes have been passing to and fro. In parts of France it must be one long Alert, day and night." **(Cox)***

TUESDAY 2nd May 1944 *"...Worked until seven on same jobs. Did some more in the shed this evening. Glued up the bookcase I have made for myself. A quieter day in the air. Very few planes seen. No news from the war fronts. This is a weary time, waiting for something to happen. All sorts of rumours come from the docks. I heard today that when the invasion takes place, all repair work etc will cease in the docks. Also, that the Bargate, which runs the sewage sludge down to the Nab, must not operate after today." **(Cox)***

FRIDAY 5th MAY 1944 *"...Worked until five o'clock. Finished off the bookcase this evening and did a good bit to Tanners. There was a warning at quarter past two this morning. I did not get up, and the "All Clear" went within ten minutes. The latest information I have regarding the invasion is that it will take place during the end of next week." **(Cox)***

SATURDAY 6th MAY 1944 *"...Worked as usual until twelve. Did a good bit to the bookcase this afternoon, and did one or two other jobs. Could not go out this evening because my sports coat is at the cleaners. No news at all at nine o'clock. When I came home at dinner time, there was a long line of very big tanks coming down Bitterne Road and buses, tradesmens vans and Army lorries were all mixed up with them, making a long jam. During the afternoon could hear the rumble of tanks going through Bitterne." **(Cox)***

SUNDAY 7th MAY 1944 *"...Was up at nine. Enjoyed breakfast. Could not go out, so went out in the shed and did some polishing until dinner was ready. Went to bed this afternoon and slept until nearly five. Spent most of the evening reading. Many squadrons of planes going over again late this afternoon and this evening, but not much after dark. There is still no news from the war fronts." **(Cox)***

WEDNESDAY 10th MAY 1944 *"...Worked until five o'clock. Some more work has come in. The conversion of two dumb barges. ...Just before dark the smoke screen on this side of the water was put into operation and Bill said it was quite thick when he came through Spring Road." **(Cox)***

SUNDAY 14th MAY 1944 *"Fine all day. Some cloud this morning. A strong cold wind blowing. Evening fine. Worked as usual all day. Did nothing in the shed this evening, but washed and changed early and sat reading in front of a good fire. Soon after 11 o'clock there was a warning. I was in bed and did not get up. The "All Clear" went without incident. During the night a second Alert sounded. I did not get up and dropped off to sleep again. I was awakened by a crash of gunfire, and saw through the window the sky to the West a mass of orange* *coloured lights, shells from the Bofers guns. With Elsie, scrambled out in a hurry, called Ted and went outside, saw a plane caught in the searchlights with all the guns in the neighbourhood letting fly at it. It went out towards the East and while watching I saw a ball of fire appear in the sky, drop slowly behind the trees and houses and a soft red glow appear across the sky. Whether it was a plane hit or a flare I know not. Later another plane came over, this time travelling East to West. Again all the Bofers opened up and there was a wonderful pyrotechnic display. The plane could be seen quite clearly in the rays of the searchlights and while the barrage was at its height there was the swish of a bomb or two and the usual dull explosion. But there was nothing after this episode, although the All Clear did not go until some time afterwards, having been in operation over an hour. The time of the warning was round about two o'clock."* **(Cox)**

MONDAY 15th MAY 1944 *"A white frost this morning. Fine all day, but cold, and lots of cloud at times. Evening overcast. Working until seven o'clock. Heard that the bombs were dropped last night at Highfield, wrecking many houses, killing five people, and wounding many others. Felt tired and cold all day and on arrival home this evening did not get out in the shed. Went to bed at half past ten and at midnight woke up and heard the sirens. Guns were firing in the distance, so I roused the family and dressed and took the chit up to the post. Just as I reached the post there was a whiz and a whine, followed by an explosion which sounded very near. There was some gunfire at the time. I gave in the chit and hurried back home. The family and Doris were in the shelter. There was lots of gunfire and the sound of several planes, but owing to the cloud could not see what was going on. Soon in the direction of Cowes the sky was full of flares. The rain continued for over an hour and it was nearly half past one before the All Clear blew. It was a very dark night and the searchlights were not much use in the clouds. During last nights raids, which were very scattered, the Germans lost fifteen planes."* **(Cox)**

(The last air raid on Southampton was on 15th May 1944, causing much damage in Portswood, with 4 people killed and 22 injured.)

WEDNESDAY 17th MAY 1944 *"Worked on some jobs until five. P.C. came in the shop just before we finished. He tells me that fifteen of the concrete barges, or Quay walls, as they are called, have been sunk somewhere in the Channel and he has to get them up. So if they are wanted for the "Invasion" what hopes have we of it coming off yet. But all the excitement of a week or two ago has died down and most people have gone back to the old thoughts that nothing will happen this summer. Spent the evening in the shed."* **(Cox)**

"Well we didn't know, we just thought it was a build-up, because they were stationed in the Common and, various areas around, you know,...I suppose the adults thought more about what it was... but we didn't think much of it, you know, we just knew there was troops on the move ... my brother-in-law, he had TB about that time ... and...my husband wanted to go down and see him... We went across to the Isle of Wight and we saw all the barges and all and I presume some of the Mulberry Docks ... we didn't know what it was for..." **(Violet Hoare)**

"It was the English troops first of all and Southampton was gradually becoming more and more of a garrison town and we were sealed off and my father's brother and sister felt they had to come down ... and we had to get permission for them to come down. I had to go down to the railway station and when they got off the train, say that they were who they were and this sort of thing, to meet them." **(Kate White)**

"... Up at the end of Aldermoor Road they covered the grass each side with brick rubble and ashes and things to make a standing ground for the tanks and this was all the way round the Rownhams area and all Nursling and all over the place and these convoys of tanks and things used to come in and move off, you know, they camouflage them, and then they'd move off and go on manouevres in the area and they'd come round again and all of a sudden one night...one morning they were gone and...then

we heard on the news that the D-Day landings had taken place and I'd slept through the night, I didn't hear the planes going over continuously with the paratroops ... " **(John Hobbs)**

"We lived in Pentire Avenue and 10 days before D-Day the place filled up with tanks, lined up on each side of the road, just left enough room for us to get in and out of our houses and first they were English boys and we used to leave the door open at night so they could come in and sleep on the floor of the sitting room instead of sleeping in the tanks...then the Americans came in and they were here much longer than the English boys.

I had a pass to get into the docks, people were encouraged not to go there, it was sort of a war zone...there wasn't much normal deck work going on, it was all military.

Everyone knew D-Day was imminent because we were full of army vehicles the month before...from here where we lived in Pentire Avenue is a mile and a half and all those roads were filled with tanks and army wagons ..." **(Harold Jackson-Seed)**

"Just shortly before the embarkation of troops, it was when there was an armed guard actually stationed there (beside Harbour Board offices) - a naval guard - that we realised something important was imminent.

At the Town Quay. Outside the actual (Harbour Board) offices there was a ramp for embarking troops and vehicles and I can remember that was when we really were scrutinised to get down to the area. You could see a lot of what we thought were barges which were the landing craft of course and there were some very big structures which I assume were part of the Mulberry Harbour but you never said - 'You see that over there - that's the Mulberry Harbour!'

I can remember that nothing was explained - it was what you picked up at the time and all you were told was TOP SECRET and you knew you read it and to all intents and purposes forgot it. Every secret letter had to go in double envelopes - the internal envelope was marked TOP SECRET and the outside envelope was just addressed to The Admiralty, Bugle Street...

There was quite a lot of - especially in the build-up to D-Day - a lot of discussion about the loading ramps and we had one built right outside the office of the Harbour Board and there were armed guards on there all the time and this was for...the landing craft assault ships and the landing craft tank ships came in to pick up the men and the tanks or armoured personnel carrier or whatever was being transported at that time!

There was all this with the building of the ramps - we knew what the ramps were for - there was also talk about PLUTO which was the Pipe-Line-Under-The-Ocean.

There were a lot of troops and everyone knew that something was going to happen and of course when D-Day occurred we knew it was fairly imminent because they whitewashed all the windows on the sea side of the Harbour Board offices so that we couldn't see what was going on. We had a jolly good idea!" **(Patricia Cameron)**

"Long before the date scheduled for the actual invasion, the docks at the Port bore testimony to the vastness of the operations involved for the accumulation of naval, and operational shipping severely taxed all available accommodation. Many vessels had to be berthed abreast, and operational craft were in places tied up seven and eight abreast. The water area of some of the wet docks seemed to be almost completely filled with landing craft, and altogether the seven miles of quays at the Docks presented an unforgettable sight.

Just prior to D-Day all commercial and Lease-Lend shipping ceased, and the Port was converted into a purely operational centre. The Prime Minister, Mr Winston Churchill, and the Minister of War Transport, Lord Leathers, visited the Port at a time when many of the British troops who were to take part in the initial assault upon the beaches of Normandy were congregated in the Docks and when ships of all types were lying at the quays already loaded with stores and equipment for the invading armies." **(Southampton Docks Handbook, 1947)**

Loading stores at Southampton Docks, 1944. (ABP)

Rocket caskets being loaded onto a rocket ship before D-Day. These rocket ships each had a battery of 75 rocket guns and were used to pound the French coast. (ABP)

Landing craft in docks, before D-Day. (ABP)

Naval craft in New Docks before D-Day. (ABP)

Torpedo casks being unloaded from a railway truck and wrapped in netting ropes for lifting. (Newfield)

"Working with civilians...tends to slow work down. They are working to put in time, soldiers are working to save time and get back to their quarters."
(14th Port Books)

Landing craft in the Empress Dock, December 1943. (ABP)

British officers on an assault ship, May 1944. (Masterton)

Assault ship and landing craft, May 1944. (Masterton)

Stores being loaded onto an assault ship, May 1944. (Masterton)

Four landing craft in dry dock, fitting out for D-Day. (ABP)

Ocean Dock, 4th June 1944. (National Archives of Canada)

American military vehicles and troops in Rockleigh Road, Southampton. (Bert Bagg)

"In the photo are my grandparents Soloman and Eliza Bagg, he owned the house 185 Hill Lane, on the corner of Hill Lane and Rockleigh Road. My mother Annie is hanging out the clothes...I was at work.

The photographer asked to use the back bedroom to take the photo, as far as I know he was a reporter from The Daily Sketch...

The Americans and the Free French were here, all packed up outside the house to go to the embarkation points, it was taken in the early part of 1944.

They were very friendly, especially when the sirens went, they were down the shelter before we were...we were immune to it after 4 years, we didn't worry.

I was born in the house, my father and mother lived there, my grandparents were 82 at the time...

We knew it was approaching D-Day but the troops never knew when they were going...

The heading of the photograph was 'War Over the Garden Wall' when it was printed.

My grandfather was a builder, in fact he was the bricklayer who built the house and then he bought it in 1901...the house is still there today, it hasn't altered much except for some modernization of the windows...he paid £320 for it..." *(Bert Bagg)*

A group of Wrens outside the South Western Hotel, taken near D-Day. Jean Lammas (later Jean Rouse) is second from the right.

"I do remember that it was all very hush-hush and most movements to the docks were made at night under the cover of heavy smoke screens. One night a friend and myself had a late pass so went to visit another friend out Bitterne way and on the way back we got caught up in one of the smoke screens and got very lost and were eventually found by a couple of MPs who escorted us back to the South Western Hotel.

As far as work was concerned it didn't make any difference much to me as I had the usual film shows of Aircraft Recognition and Eye Shooting to give to the D.E.M.S. and Merchant Navy boys, although a few days prior to D-Day all the male staff were taken away to work on the guns in ships at the docks so I was left in charge of the office."*(Jean Rouse)*

SATURDAY 27th MAY 1944 "A fine lovely hot day. Evening same. Was up at nine and after breakfast went out in the shed and attempted to finish off the fire screen for Iris. But I could not get the linen stretched tight enough and although I was on the job until dinner time, I had to leave it unfinished in the end. Had a short doze after dinner. Joe came in during the afternoon and since I was glad of an excuse to pack up work I washed and changed and I borrowed Ted's bike and we rode out to Durley Church to have a look at the Yew tree which stands outside. A very pleasant ride although it was rather hot. Don came up after tea, with the baby, and when he went Elsie and I went for a walk through the woods at the back of Glenfield round old Bitterne and so home. Went to bed at eleven. The sirens went after midnight. I took the chit up to the post. It was very quiet here, although once or twice there was a distant rumble of gunfire. The All Clear went without incident." *(Cox)*

WHITSUNDAY 28th MAY 1944 "Fine and hot again all day. Evening same. Was up at nine again this morning and after breakfast washed and changed and soon after ten Joe came round. We walked through Cutbushes to Woodmill, along the two path and home via Manor Farm Road. When we got back to Bitterne we found The Angel shut so we walked on up to The Fox & Hounds but this was closed, as was The Firs also. But fortunately we found The Brewery open and after a struggle had two pints of Bass, which made me sweat. After dinner I went out in the garden, threw myself down on some old cushions and went to sleep for a couple of hours. Went for a walk with Elsie this evening round Weston and through Mayfield. We passed lots of pubs, but they were all closed. All day long much air activity and before midnight there was a warning. Heard gunfire very far away but nothing here and the Alert was over within half an hour. But just before two there was a second Alert. The danger signal went, but nothing developed here although the warning was on for an hour." *(Cox)*

TUESDAY 30th May 1944 "...Restarted work this morning. Some more rush jobs. Twelve notice boards for Sea Transport wanted in a hurry and four hundred more parting boards. E.M. went to Redhill this afternoon to bring back the ply. I stopped until six this evening. Had a telephone message from Edgar May this afternoon telling me that Eddie and Ethel have been bombed out at Park Gate. During the second Alert last night a plane dropped a couple of bombs on a tank by the side of the road and set it on fire. This in turn set other tanks on fire and the ammo inside exploded in all directions. Ted rode out on his bike this evening and he said that the house is completely wrecked, and the surrounding district has the appearance of a battlefield, with wrecked tanks strewn around and shells and debris lying on the ground. Eddie and Ethel and Brenda are uninjured." *(Cox)*

The Echo reported heavy bombing raids on the French Coast in the days of early June before D-Day.

SATURDAY 3rd JUNE 1944 *"Dull most of the day. Some bright periods. Evening fine but cloudy and threatening. Worked as usual until twelve. On my way home was held up by a long convoy which stretched right up Cobbett Road, Lances Hill and as far as I could see up Bursledon Road. No traffic was allowed down Lances Hill. Had my usual after dinner doze and then went out in the shed but only messed about with the lathe. I came in at half past three and sat listening to a radio programme until five o'clock. Did nothing this evening. I felt tired and had a burning at the back of my nose and throat and my head felt heavy. Heard a rumour this afternoon that Allied forces had attacked and captured the Channel Islands. I expect many rumours during the next week or two. Many people heard heavy but distant gunfire during last night but it did not disturb me."* **(Cox)**

SUNDAY 4th JUNE 1944 *"Dull this morning. Bright periods this afternoon, with strong winds. It became cloudy again this evening and rain commenced later, being blown along by strong wind. The rain did not develop into heavy downpour. Cold. Worked until 5 o'clock. A day of rumours. We are supposed to have landed on the North Coast of France and the rumour regarding the Channel Islands is very persistent. Suffered all day from a violent cold, which has pitched in my head. Did nothing this evening but lop in the armchair in front of the fire. A warning this evening without incidents."* **(Cox)**.

MONDAY 5th JUNE 1944 *"Another dull miserable day with a flurry of rain at times. A nasty cold wind. Evening dull. Some patches of blue sky. Worked until seven o'clock on some jobs but work is getting scarce again and E.M. says that overtime will have to finish unless something crops up. Some firms are sending men home after they have booked on. My cold is very bad and when I got home I felt lousy and when I went to bed I had a glass of hot milk and some Aspro's. This mornings news is that the Allies have entered Rome. The city seems to have been taken without much inside opposition and the buildings etc have not been damaged."* **(Cox)**

D-Day - 6th June 1944

British troops boarding the assault ship SS Empire Lance on 29th May 1944, ready for D-DAY.
(Imperial War Museum B5237)

Commandoes from the 1st Special Service Brigade boarding landing craft at Warsash, 3rd June 1944.
(Imperial War Museum H39043 and H39044)

**British Infantry coming ashore at Gold Beach in Normandy, 7th June 1944.
(Imperial War Museum B5245)**

In the assault phase of Operation Overlord, Southampton was the embarkation port for the British and Canadian forces. Two-thirds of the entire British Assault Force passed through Southampton. These were the UK Force G, which landed on Gold Beach, and Force J which landed on Juno Beach. Force G included troops from the 1st Battalion, Hampshire Regiment, part of the 50th (Northumbrian) Division. Other British troops left from Portsmouth and ports in Sussex. The American assault forces left from Poole and ports in Dorset and the West Country.

Bad weather delayed the launching of the invasion by one day but when the forecast for June 6th was reasonable, that day was chosen as D-Day.

On Monday June 5th, the fleet left Southampton and headed for the assembly point off the Isle of Wight.

A total of 156,000 troops landed in Normandy on D-Day, of which nearly 10,000 took part in the first wave of landings. 7,000 ships were involved, including 4,026 landing craft. 10,000 aircraft were used to carry airborne troops and bombard the coast.

A prayer service was held in the ruins of St. Mary's Church on the evening of D-Day - attended by Mayor Cll. R. J. Stranger.

SO'TON A.T.S. RECEIVED FIRST INVASION NEWS

Nine A.T.S. Signals operators gave the world the news that D-Day had arrived. Soon after they came on duty at the Supreme Headquarters of the Allied Expeditionary Forces - a message was handed in at the receiving hatch of the signal office which is staffed by men and women of the British and American Services. It was General Eisenhower's first communique.

The first person to read it was Lance Corporal Mary Parry, of Southampton, 24 years old, wife of a R.E.M.E. craftsman serving in Italy. When she found it contained news of Allied landings in France, her first thought was "How awful it would be if I made a mistake." She quickly routed it for registration.

From there the communique went to the teleprinter room, where seven A.T.S. operators simultaneously transmitted it to the War Cabinet and Allied H.Q. all over the world.

The whole shift were delighted that they happened to be on duty when the No.1 invasion communique came through. Some of the most confidential clerks had known for some hours that the operations had begun, and immediately the communique was issued everyone in the camp was handed a personal message from General Eisenhower - the same message that was given to each member of the Expeditionary Force.

All A.T.S. serving with S.H.A.E.F. - and there are several hundreds of them - have been specially chosen for their efficiency, good conduct and personal integrity. They work side by side with members of all three Services - both British and American.

They enjoy living in a camp run on American lines under a W.A.C. officer, and share W.A.C. barrack rooms, mess with them, and are on U.S. rations cooked by W.A.C. cooks. They even drill to American words of command.

All efforts by the "Echo" to trace the home address of L. Cpl. Parry have so far not been successful.

(Echo, 12th June 1944)

TUESDAY 6th JUNE 1944 "Not so much improvement in the weather. Dull and cold most of the day. Some bright periods. Evening overcast. Well I have to record it at last. Today is D day. The Allies invaded France this morning, landing men and tanks etc in Normandy. A queer day. I woke up once or twice during the night and heard the roar of planes but did not take much notice. But when I went to work the sky was full of planes, bunches of heavy bombers passing over in many directions. And as men began to come into the shop it was remarked that perhaps the invasion had started. Soon after eight o'clock the first rumours began to circulate and as the office people came in it was confirmed that we had begun the assault on Europe. But there was not much excitement. At ten o'clock, and again at eleven, I heard on the radio the announcement of our landings. Things were quiet throughout the day and at nine o'clock this evening the King broadcast a message. The news which followed was pretty well the same as the morning bulletins. I don't expect much news for a few days. Between eight and nine this evening saw many planes towing gliders pass over. Otherwise the day has been singularly free from air and road activity. Worked until seven o'clock on some jobs. My cold still bad. On arrival home washed and changed and with Elsie went round and saw Pomeroy the A.R.P chief regarding Elsies' fire watching. He said that it would only be necessary to sign at Whites Road Post every eight days and after signing she could return home. So having settled that we hurried back to listen to the radio, had supper and went to bed early with a thought for those fighting on the other side."
(Cox)

"6 June 1944 - D-Day - made tea, took my shutters down. Quiet day. Cold. Very little sunshine."
(Diary of Gertrude White)

"I supervised the fire guard for the whole of the Civic Centre and took my turn of duty, and the evening of 5th June 1944 I was on duty, two of us went for a stroll to get some fresh air instead of being in the basement all the time, the siren hadn't gone, no warning, we looked up in the sky and it was literally full of aeroplanes with about 8 gliders *behind, and the sky was full of these things, and we stood and looked at each other and I said "Hey mate it's tomorrow", these were the gliders going over to do the softening up ...and during the early hours of the morning there was a dickens of a row in Pentire Avenue and all the tanks had gone, everything had gone...and when they were in Germany some of the Americans used to write to us, if they could give an English address they could get leave, and they would come and stay with us for a few days."* (**Harold Jackson-Seed**)

"When I first came to Southampton, was just prior to the invasion on the 6th June 1944...I was just 18...how I come first to be in Southampton - I came round here by ship in one of these specially built landing ships for the Normandy Invasion which as you know was on 6th June. Well the ship I was on was called the Empire Broadsword and after our third run over to France we got blown up and the ship was sunk and I was landed ashore in Southampton.

The 'Broadsword' was one of these Liberty type ships, I believe she was built in about ten days...we could do about 12 or 14 knots and we had twelve Landing Craft Assaults each side so we could get three thousand off in about three minutes...They hung on the davits you put troops in there, you drop into the sea and these LCAs go right up on the beach!

Well...the only difference in her compared to ships in them days was a funny shaped sort of a funnel, it didn't have derricks and stuff like ordinary cargo boats because she was specially designed for the invasion and when you say come to Southampton there was quite a few of them... We're all ready for D-Day and course we sail and anchor in the Solent, waiting to start, we got bombed that night...when I say bombed there was the German airforce attacking us all round, then we went to sea, we went to a place which is west of Caen, now I'll never forget going across there, because the Chaplain he had us all up on deck and he said the last prayer and all this...everybody said 'Christ what's gonna happen here?'...." (**Wally Walton**)

"D-Day itself was full of excitement and apprehension. I recall that in the afternoon when the first hospital ships arrived bringing in American wounded and they transferred to waiting trains at South Western Station they were greeted by a U.S. Army band playing the Stars & Stripes. This went on night and day for nearly a week and drove the occupants of the South Western Hotel nearly mad.

In the evenings I did a bit of canteen work on the station, handing out cups of tea and cigarettes to the wounded. Quite an eye-opener and made one think how futile war could be." (**Jean Rouse**)

AFTER D-DAY

In the weeks and months following D-Day, Southampton became the port of embarkation for troops crossing to France to reinforce the armies there. Between D-Day and the end of the war, about 3.5 million service personnel passed through the port to France. Over two million of these were Americans, and convoys of American troops and vehicles became a familiar sight in the town. Military equipment and stores were shipped from the port. In the 17 weeks following the invasion, the port handled a cargo tonnage greater than the whole import and export tonnage handled in 1938. In all, 60% of the American troops and equipment shipped from British ports to the continent, went from Southampton.

"Day after day for fourteen months, truck-load after truck-load, column after column, of white and coloured troops surged through the town, and entering dockland, were lost to sight. It was a poignant scene. Inexpressibly inspiring, it was as inexpressibly sad. Neither among the townspeople nor the troops themselves was there any appearance of levity. There were no flags, no drums, no music, no huzzahing. Every citizen without exception seemed to be awed into silence by the gravity and immensity of the occasion." **(Knowles)**

American troops march past Gods House Tower. (Newfield)

American troops with baggage. (Newfield)

Berth Location Board. (Newfield)

American army lorries loaded with troops entering the Old Docks. (Newfield)

American soldiers in the docks in 1944. (ABP)

American troops embarking for Normandy. (Newfield)

Convoy awaiting shipment to France at No. 10 Gate in the New Docks, 13th June 1944. (ABP)

Southampton Docks, 13th June 1944. (ABP)

American port company soldiers using a fork-lift truck, 14th June 1944. (ABP)

There was a shortage of cranes and mechanical equipment in the port before the arrival of the Americans. The 14th Port brought with them their own equipment, including prefabricated cranes and fork-lift trucks. The fork-lift trucks were new to the port and seem to have caused some interest. Joy riding was a problem.

American convoy arriving at Southampton Docks for shipment to the continent, 4th July 1944. Note the woman bumper driver. (ABP)

Loading stores for Normandy in the New Docks, 4th July 1944. (ABP)

Vehicles being loaded onto the "Abiel Foster" for shipment to the continent, 4th July 1944. (ABP)

American soldiers loading vehicles onto the "George Steers" in the New Docks, 4th July 1944. (ABP)

American lorry being hoisted aboard a US Motor Transport Vessel. These MTVs were former Liberty ships converted into vehicle ferries for the cross-channel voyage. Many were converted in Southampton yards prior to D-Day. (Echo)

Scrambling nets being loaded by American soldiers, 4th July 1944. (ABP)

American army convoy. (Newfield)

Loading a heavy armoured vehicle at Northam Docks. (Newfield)

Two large missiles on American trailer trucks. (Newfield)

American soldiers working on a lorry chassis. (Newfield)

American army personnel in the docks. (Newfield)

American army vehicles on Town Quay. The Harbour Board Office is in the background. (Newfield)

American lorry being driven onto a landing craft at Town Quay. (Newfield)

WEDNESDAY 7th JUNE 1944 *"Dull again this morning, with a shower of rain first thing. It improved this afternoon and was much warmer but clouded up again this evening. Not so much wind. Worked until five o'clock. After tea, feeling heavy I dropped off to sleep for a time and then rose and went out in the shed and soled two pairs of shoes. The war news about the same. Our beachheads consolidated. Not much air activity today."* **(Cox)**

THURSDAY 8th JUNE 1944 *"Dull and cloudy again this morning. A light steady rain set in this afternoon and continued until mid evening. Cloudy but fine later. Worked until seven o'clock. Did nothing in the shed on arrival home. Listened to the last "Itma" programme. Not a lot of news at nine o'clock. There were lots of planes passing over this morning and men working at the docks say that many wounded are coming back and also some German prisoners. There was a warning early this morning, but it was very short and I did not have time to light my pipe before the "All Clear" sounded."* **(Cox)**

10th JUNE 1944 - Regal Cinema weekly return. Showing "The Sullivans" and "Lucky Days". *"First feature very powerful. Created tremendous interest and would, I am sure, have made terrific returns had it not been for D-Day, which affected this town very considerably. Second feature considered adequate support."* **(T. Lowe, Manager)**

SUNDAY 18th JUNE 1944 *"Fine all day but some cloud at times with a thundery tendency. Evening same. Worked until five o'clock. Went for a walk with Elsie after tea, through Mayfield and Weston and along the shore. The shore's in a terrible state, with packing cases, iron beams and tanks and all sorts of debris littering the beach. It was on the beach that many landing flats were put together and launched. As we were walking back in Archery Road the siren sounded. Despite the threats of the flying bomb nobody took the slightest notice of the warning and it passed without incident. There was also a warning at quarter past five this morning. Soon after midnight the sirens sounded again. I took the chit up to the post. Beyond some flashes which I took to be sheet lightning, nothing happened and the All Clear went before I got home. Todays news is that the Cherbourg Peninsula has been cut by American Troops and about 25,000 Germans are trapped. In other places in France bitter fighting is taking place but not a lot of progress being made yet."* **(Cox)**

SUNDAY 9th JULY 1944 *"...Worked all day on some jobs, bored and fed up. After tea, had a short doze and since the weather was so bad did not go out, but polished the workbox I made. Tonight was announced the capture of Caen by our troops. The Americans are also making progress on the other front. But it seems so slow. There was a warning at one o'clock this morning and I had just left home to *go to the Post, when the All Clear sounded, so I returned to bed at once." **(Cox)***

15th JULY 1944 - Regal Cinema weekly return. Showing "Melody Inn" and "Timber Queen". Attendances were affected by *"several nights of flying bombs..."*

29th JULY - Regal Cinema weekly return. Showing "Tender Comrade" and "Tornado." *"A feature with a strong, sentimental appeal to American visitors to this country. English not so much impressed." **(A. New, Manager)***

SUNDAY 3rd SEPTEMBER 1944 *"...Most of the newspapers this morning printed sensational reports that American troops had crossed into Germany but there was no official confirmation at nine o'clock this evening. Troops have crossed into Belgium and everywhere the Germans are reported to be retreating in disorder." **(Cox)***

Kate White talking to American troops camped outside her home in Melrose Road, Shirley.

"Dad was a great rose grower, we had over a hundred in the garden. Bushes, standard roses and a couple of climbers, they were just coming out, some in bud and some in full bloom so Dad stripped the garden and gave them to the soldiers, they put them on their tanks and on their hats. I remember it being mentioned on the later newsreels and in the newspapers that the red rose of England was going back to France."

*(The Americans were) "kindness in themselves, they were so good with children who, had time for them and of course they were just awaiting for transport to go away and they were miles away from home and friends and they were only too grateful for people to open their houses, and our front door and back door was open all the time; they were just in and out. The lady of the house, they sat with her, they talked to her." **(Kate White)***

*"Certainly around here (Shirley Warren) near to the main Winchester Road there you saw all the troops being moved to the docks, they all came along Winchester Road...thousands of them!." **(Michael Hunt)***

"They used to often set up a field kitchen in the docks if they had a number of troops arrive...we often ate soup and a bit of bread, fresh cooked American donuts through the generosity of the American forces...

I think they found coming in to the war environment a little bit shattering. We'd I suppose gradually developed with it - it wasn't so bad for us. But coming from America straight into a war environment I think it was a bit much for some of them and the occasional air raid we had with the Americans about, which gave them their first taste of war...I'm sure they found them rather shattering!

*They came in a lot of them into the Common and bivouac'd for the night and then marched down through the town. Sometimes they were kept hanging about - if they could go straight on board it was all right. I do remember several groups arriving that looked as though they wanted freshening up so we used to open up our little washing facility and let them make use of it and they were always most grateful! Two things tickled me - they would very quickly form a line or queue if you like and there was no pecking order - there was the privates and the N.C.O.'s and they were all mixed up together and patiently took their turn." **(Jimmy Mead)***

"When the Americans left I looked in our front garden and there was a jerry can at the back of the garden wall, it was petrol, they left it as a present for me...but my near neighbour was a police sergeant...he said 'that's very dangerous having that old boy I'd better take it', so I said 'what are you going to do with it'. 'Well', he said, 'I can't get enough petrol to keep the lawns mown up at the police hostel', so I lost my 5 gallons."
(Harold Jackson-Seed)

"I was a foreman in charge of...shipping tanks and guns and half track vehicles at 102 berth. One night we were loading...my job was loading these Liberty ships with the tanks and guns and things...and it all had to be shipped by the ships derricks, because the theory was that the Germans wouldn't leave any cranes for us to work over on the French coast, so we had to lift all the equipment up with the ships' gear, because when they reached the German coast they had to unload by the same means...so I was the foreman...one night we were doing this...I was all on my own, working...these Liberty ships had five hatches and...I was watching number two hatch in particular because number two hatch was the big hatch that took Sherman tanks...they weighed about forty-five tonnes...in number four hatch, the hatch I'm gonna talk about, they had shipped half track vehicles...they weighed about twelve tonnes and remember, we had to do it all...this was working at night...we had to do all this in the blackout...and the only light we had was a forty watt bulb hanging over the side of the ship and you can imagine was not very much...and...the labourer I had that night was an American labourer because there weren't enough Southampton dockers to work the ships so the Americans had their own labour force and that particular night they sent me all these American men...and...all due credit to them...they tried hard but they weren't used to this kind of work. ....During the night, somewhere round about three o'clock in the morning they were working...lifting a half track vehicle up at number four hatch...and...I was listening to the sounds...I could tell by the sounds if things were going right...and I suddenly stopped for a moment listening...and I ran as fast as I could towards number four, I shouted to the men on the quay "Run! Run for your life, run!" and they all scattered...and then CRASH! Down came this half track vehicle onto the quay...obviously had the men not run or me as well...obviously we'd have been crushed completely... I went to see the American Officer about this and...he wasn't really interested, he was sound asleep, anyway, I woke him up and I told him "you gotta come out and have a look at this"...he came out "Oh dear" he said "sweep it away", I said "what do you mean 'sweep it away', how can you sweep away twelve tons of rubbish like this?!" He said " ...get a bulldozer"...well, we'd never heard of bulldozers then, all right they had them in America, but we didn't have them so I said "we haven't got bulldozers either". So we had to leave it till the morning...in the morning along came some more American staff to clear up all this mess and...one of the men was in a bomb disposal squad...he said "what happened here?", so I told him. He said "wasn't there any sparks?". I said "it was like bonfire night, this vehicle came straight down, scraped the side...well you can see where it scraped the side of the ship and...sparks all over the place". He said "you're lucky, that vehicle was packed tight with high explosive. By rights that should have gone off and blown you and the ship to blazes, and half of Southampton as well."
(Frank Barrett)

"The weeks wore on, still the tanks continued to throw down their 'E' rations, their cigarettes and their money. Because of the continual build-up of traffic, for reasons best known to the powers that were, every few hours the dock gates would have to be closed. As the docks were overflowing with the military, convoys of troops and equipment had to wait in the street for hours, sometimes all day.

All the kids used to climb over the jeeps and lorries, all the ammunition was there, it was all covered in canvas then but we used to lift it up and have a look, kids would get anywhere." **(Marion Ainsworth)**

"....Many times, a GI leaning over the side of his lorry, would ask me if I could fetch him something to drink. Once I answered that I had nothing to carry the drink in. Stretching down the soldier handed me his helmet. Dashing into the nearest pub's snug bar I managed to get the helmet filled with beer. Usually when a convoy was moving slowly, an officer would be walking beside one of the vehicles, and as I reached up on tip-toe an officer marched briskly up to me, and calmly taking the container away from me, poured the liquid down the drain.

....I used to get fish and chips for them. Often when I brought it back the convoy had moved on so I sold it to another convoy. I'd already been paid for it, paid about three times over ... I was quite rich ... from the bombed buildings there was all the planks of wood there. We used to chop them up and go round all the doors and sell them a bath full of wood for 3d...." **(Marion Ainsworth)**

(As a child during the war, Marion lived in Threefield Lane, Southampton.)

Captain Hancock, DSO, Master of the "Twickenham Ferry", August 1944. (BN Pool)

After the capture of Cherbourg on 27th June 1944, a train ferry service was established to Cherbourg from west of the King George V Dry Dock in Millbrook. The first ferry to go was the Southern Railways steamer "Twickenham Ferry", carrying a complete goods train. Another of the ferries was the "Hampton Ferry" shown here.

The "Hampton Ferry" leaving for Cherbourg with rolling stock, 12th August 1944. (ABP)

Railway trucks being loaded for France, August 1944. (BN Pool)

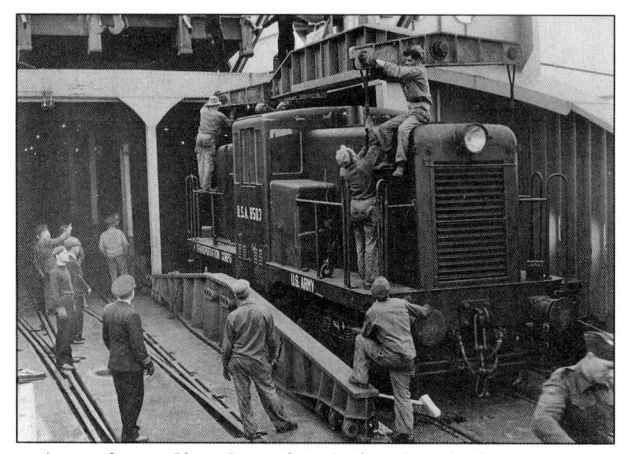

American diesel engine being loaded onto the Hampton Ferry for France. (ABP)

American troops arriving at Southampton for transit to Western Europe, 10th October 1944. (ABP)

American army women arriving at Southampton Docks.

The Millionth Yank

On October 25th 1944 the 14th Port arranged a ceremony in the docks when the millionth American soldier embarked for France. The soldier was picked out as he walked through a floral arch, a counting machine having registered "one million". He was a 26 year old infantryman, Private Paul S. Shimer of the 15th Infantry, 3rd Division of the 7th Army. The Mayor of Southampton, Mr. RJ Stranger presented him with a plaque "The Millionth Yank" and, after a private conversation with the mayor, Shimer was led away for more photographs and "the agony of an impromptu speech" (American Weekly, 1947).

Paul Shimer came from Chambersburg in Pennsylvania, and had a wife, Marion, and daughter, Patricia Ann, who was three years old in October 1944. His parents lived in McConnellsburg, Pennsylvania, his home town. Before the war, he had been assistant manager of a chain store, the J.C. Penney Company. He was inducted into the army on 19th April 1944 and left for England in October 1944. Paul Shimer later became a sergeant. He was killed in action in Germany on 14th April 1945.

Paul Shimer's brother, also a GI, was on the gang plank a few feet away when Mayor Stranger shook hands with the two millionth American to embark from the port for France on 16th January 1945.

In 1947, RJ Stranger and his wife visited America, and met Paul Shimer's family. The former mayor had started a trust fund in England towards the education of Patricia. Chambersburg, in an apple growing district, gave many gifts of apples and other foods to Southampton schools.

"They arrived in big numbers and I well remember two incidents in the docks, directly behind where we were working was an American soldier being stood up on a box being congratulated by all sorts of top brass with a placard round his neck 'One Millionth Yank' and then later on it was the 'Two Millionth Yank'. This was the mark of the number of Americans who passed through on their way to France!" **(Jimmy Mead)**

The Former mayor, RJ Stranger being interviewed by the Empire Broadcasting Corporation in New York, on Sunday 1st June 1947:-

"I was down at the docks at Southampton one morning to watch the ships, the ships that took the Americans and the British into the fighting across the Channel. I always tried to be around to wish the men good luck, but this particular morning I was waiting for the man who would be the one millionth Yank to leave Southampton for the Battle of Europe. The olive drab line marched past me up the gang plank and then one man a sergeant was called out. He was the millionth Yank. We had our picture taken together. It all happened so quickly that we didn't have much time to talk. I didn't even get his name, but I do remember he said he had a wife and baby girl at home. I told him to come back and visit my wife and me and I would help him to start his daughter in life. He said he would and then he was gone. .... I never saw that man again. United States Army Headquarters told me that he was Sergeant Paul Ed. Shimer of Chambersburg, Pennsylvania, and that he had been killed in action advancing into Germany..." **(SRO D/Z 428)**

"The Millionth Yank" ceremony in Southampton Docks, 25th October 1944. (ABP)

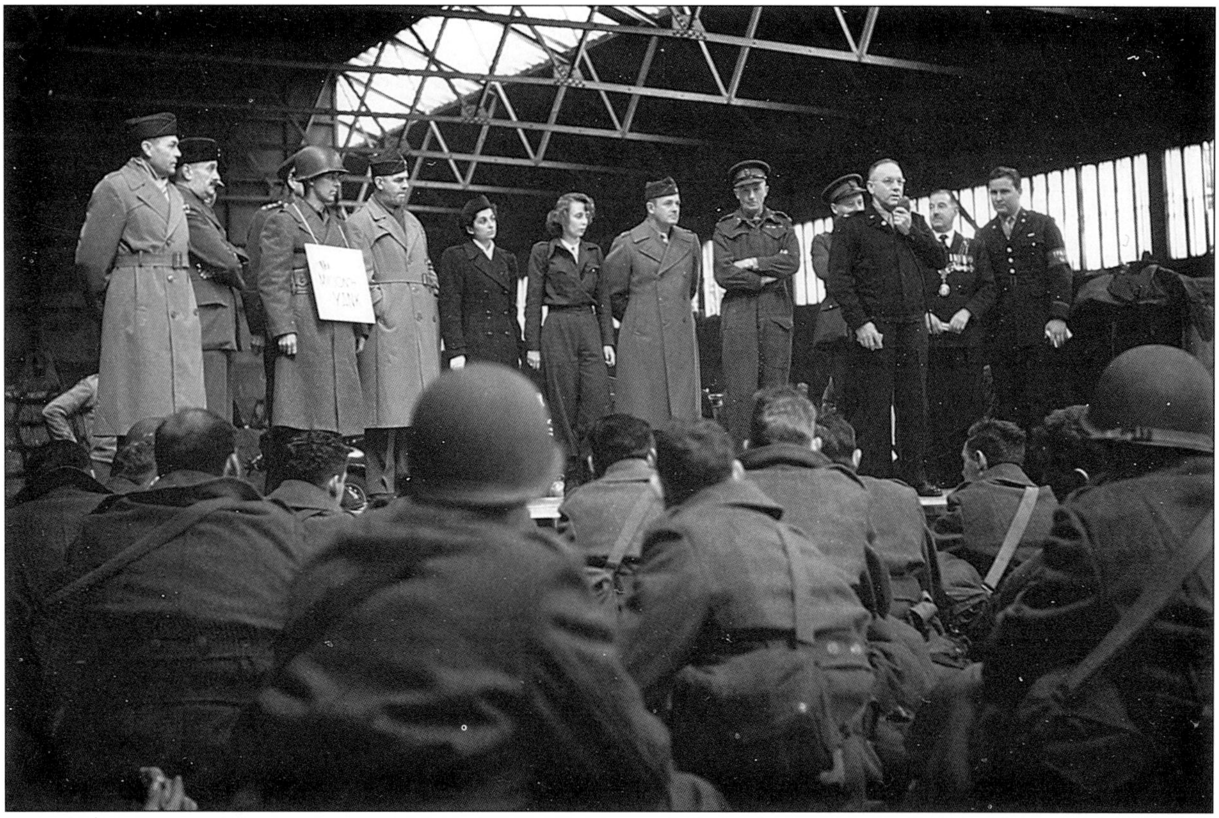

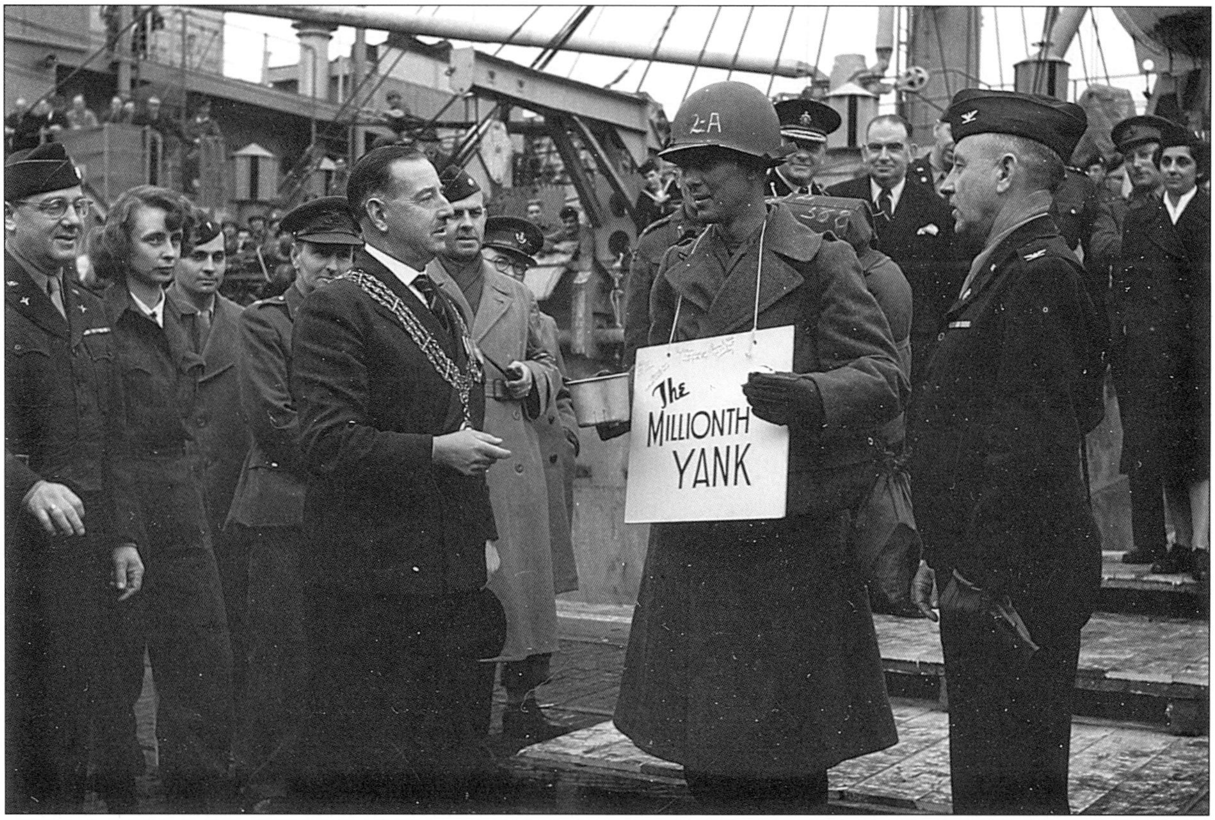
The
MILLIONTH
YANK

Part of a sermon read by the Rev. W. Wilson Carvell at the St. John's Evangelical and Reformed Church in Chambersburg, Pennsylvania, on 8th June 1947. He is talking about an address made at a banquet in Chambersburg by the former Southampton Mayor, R.J. Stranger:-

"...he described the wonderful relations that existed between the hundreds of thousands of our boys stationed there and the citizenry of Southampton. They were all waiting for D-Day. Tanks were parked along the streets everywhere. There were many dress-rehearsals. Many a morning, both the boys and residents thought that this would be the big day. So Southamptoners staged little farewell parties out of their scant supplies which they had stored away. They drank tea together. On milder days the boys would sleep right out in the open, on the sidewalks, next to their tanks. Col. Leo J. Meyer, Commanding Officer of the U.S. Army in that city, once had not slept for three straight days. He fell asleep in the garden of the home of the Mayor and Mrs. Stranger. When he awoke, he found himself in a nice soft bed. He had been carried there by those good people. That happened to many of our soldier boys." **(SRO D/Z 472)**

Private Paul S. Shimer embarking in Southampton Docks, 25th October 1944. (ABP)

Allied and German wounded began to arrive in Southampton soon after D-Day.

Wounded arriving in the port, 14th June 1944. A total of 426 hospital trains left the port after D-Day. (ABP)

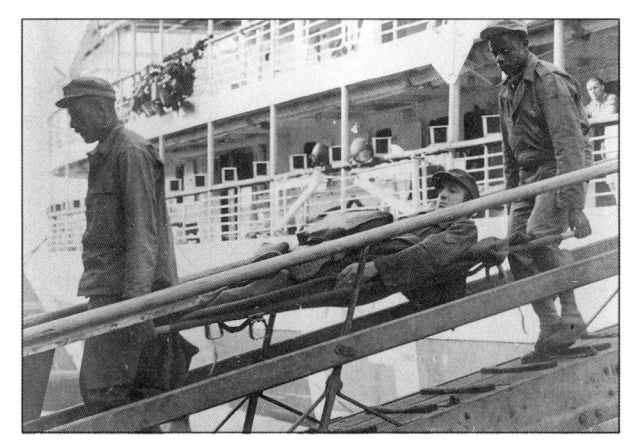

German wounded arriving in the port in May 1945. (Echo)

Prisoners of War

The first prisoners of war arrived soon after D-Day. A POW "cage", or transit camp had been set up on land in the New Docks. Here the prisoners received first-aid before being moved to more permanent camps inland. In total, 185,273 POWs entered the port after D-Day, in 315 trains. Many of them were wounded.

"VELL VE HAF COME"
- Even German Prisoners are Happy

A trainload of German prisoners passing from the coast north, today, stopped for a few moments at a south of England town. One onlooker on the platform addressed a German looking out of one of the carriage windows.

"Well Jerry, what do you think of England?" He asked.

Another German thrust his head quickly out of the window and answered in broken English: "Three years ago," he said, "Herr Hitler promised we come to England." He shrugged and placed both of his fists together as if they were handcuffed. "Vell," he added, grimly, "Ve haf come."

This lot looked exceptionally young, average age about twenty, and all were wearing soft peak service caps.

There wasn't a steel helmet among them. Their clothes looked exceptionally clean and tidy, and did not give the impression of men fresh from the battlefield. It was rather as if they had just come off a ceremonial parade.

Later another trainload passed through the town which appeared to be loaded with officers only and they were waving cheerfully and appeared to be very happy.

(Echo, 10th June 1944)

"Well, we knew that they were...Germans...that had been captured ...we just had to go and have a look at them and...you know whether we thought they had two heads and four arms I don't know but we just used to go up...you know, they would speak to the children. We were never stopped from speaking to them, a few of them spoke good English...I can remember one, especially, he was a little tiny chap and of course they used to ask us our names, and I said, you know, "What's your name?" and he said his name was August, or Au-gust (emphasis on the gust). I said "That's not a name, that's a month!". They did building work, they built the prefabs...and they did road work... and street sweeping, that sort of thing. They were allowed out of their camps, and people were asked if they would invite them into their homes, that sort of thing...but whether anybody ever did...I don't know.....

But I remember the Germans...and there were a few Italians...but not many, but there were a lot of Germans... we used to just go up and have a look at them, curiosity, you know...I mean, not like with the Americans, if you went down to the American camp you got gum and sweets and a piece of cake and, anything that was going, but with the Germans it was just curiosity." **(Dorothy Harmsworth)**

"Yes, yes funny enough there was a camp near the Common, German prisoners of war and they used to come to our off-licence - a group of them, and just sort of buy crates of beer just to take back to the camp, and my father became very friendly with two of them, and it so happened that they were carpenters. That was their trade before the war and they made my father a cabinet, a bookcase cabinet, and I think my mother only got rid of it a few years ago and we always called it the German cabinet and it was in pride of place in our home really. We kept it for a long time."
(Pamela Humphrey)

POWs arriving from France, by the Royal Pier. (Echo)

POWs in Southampton, 6th-8th June 1944. (City Heritage Collections)

General Von Shlieben, the captured German commander of Cherbourg, being brought ashore from an LST at one of the Hards, June/July 1944. (ABP)

Entrance to the transit camp for POWs near 101 Berth in the New Docks, 11th September 1944. (ABP)

Transit camp for POWs near 101 Berth, 11th September 1944. (ABP)

POWs walking to the transit camp near 101 Berth, 11th September 1944. (ABP)

POWs in the camp near 101 Berth, 13th October 1944. (ABP)

**POWs arriving from France, adjacent the to Royal Pier, March 1945.
(City Heritage Collections)**

German Generals arriving from France, 11th May 1945. (ABP)

Prisoners of War arriving at a small railway station, guarded by American 14th Port personnel. (Newfield)

Prisoners of War marching towards a camp outside Southampton. (Newfield)

Theft of Cargoes

The 14th Port Book records that losses of stores in the port due to theft were "remarkably light", although unguarded items were liable to be stolen. The docks were sealed off from the town by fences, and the Southern Railway police enforced a pass system. Unarmed guards watched cargo-handling in the docks.

"In this port, civilian stevedores have refused to work if armed guards were placed in the hold with them." **(14th Port Books)**

Among the items stolen were alcohol, drugs and officers' bedding rolls. Leather seat covers were cut away from command cars parked in the dock area, and car batteries taken. Both civilians and service personnel were thought to be responsible.

"On 1 November, a freight car on the siding near the Town Quay, was found to have been broken into and quantity of five (5) cases of twelve (12) bottles each of whiskey had been stolen."

"On 11 November, a freight car, was found unsealed and opened at shed 44 for unloading was found to have been entered and the contents (Officers' bedding rolls and foot lockers) had been tampered with and pilfered." **(14th Port Books)**

Three American Military Policemen. (Newfield)

14th Port Provost Marshal, Captain Dalton Newfield at work. (Newfield)

The 14th Port Military Police were based in Nissen Huts on Hoglands Park. The camp was known as "Hut City" by the locals.

"...have you ever heard of the Snowdrops? That was the American police...we called them Snowdrops because they had white helmets on, Snowdrops. They had great long truncheons and they used to use them too. Often we used to go out as police with them and they didn't mess about. They went into a pub where there was any trouble and bang, bang, they just knocked down and asked questions afterwards. Just different from us, you see." **(Harry Meacham)**

The entrance to the 14th Port HQ on Hoglands Park. Three American Military Policemen with Captain Dalton Newfield, the 14th Port Provost Marshal. (Newfield)

"Dal with his army and civilian crew" outside the Provost Marshal's office, Hoglands Park.
Captain Dalton Newfield is on the left. (Newfield)

"HQ by the park opposite Edwin Jones. We used to eat here a lot - girlfriends - and all."
Nissen hut canteen on Hoglands Park. (Newfield)

American soldiers and MPs, on Hoglands Park. (Newfield)

Location Board in the 14th Port HQ, Hoglands Park. (Newfield)

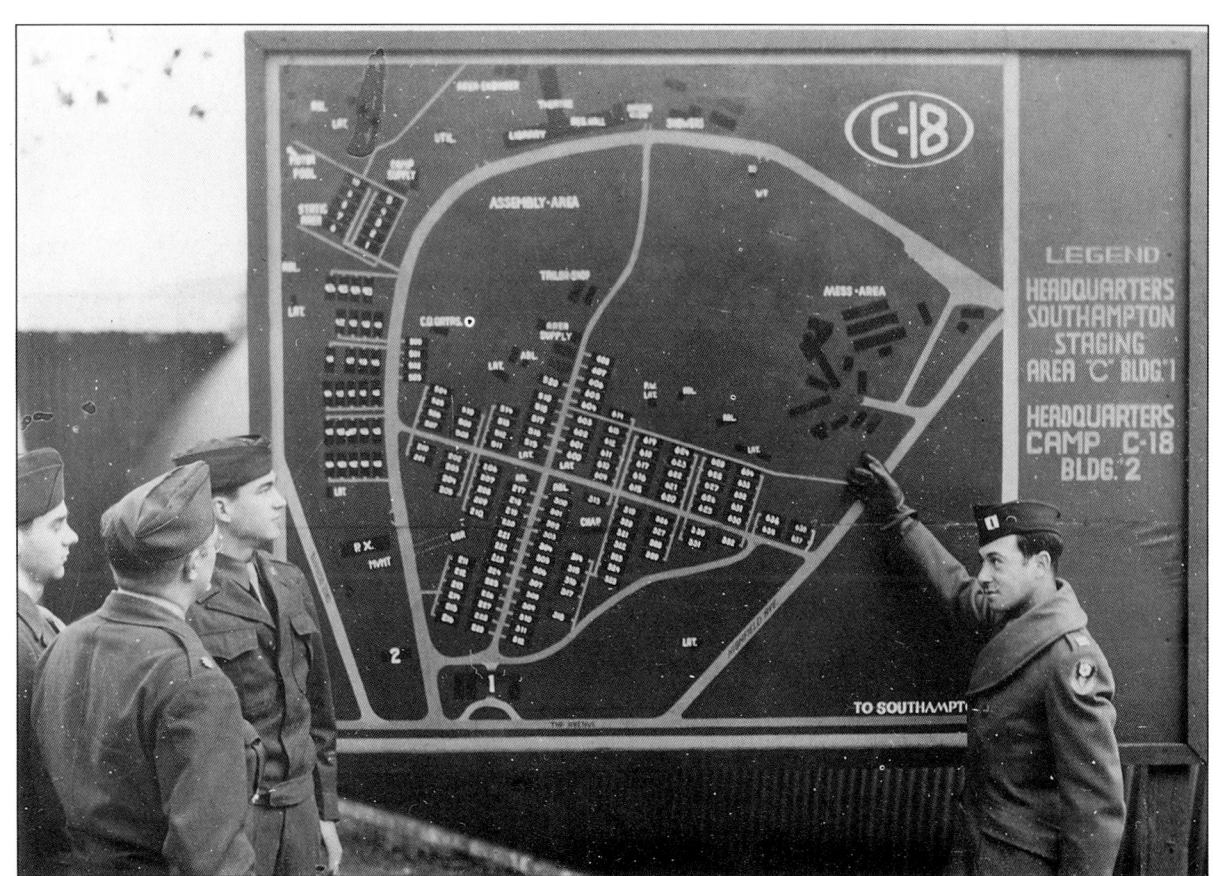

14th Port personnel with a plan of Area "C" Staging Camp C-18 on Southampton Common. (Newfield)

The 14th Port Book gives details of a "winterization" programme that was carried out in Camps C18 and C19 on Southampton Common in late 1944. These camps, unlike others in Area "C", had been set up under strict camouflage conditions, and were not of a sufficient standard to withstand wet weather. The summer of 1944 was very wet and the camp was almost uninhabitable, with mud over one foot deep.

> *"Neither can I praise too highly all that has been, and is still being done by the Southampton Division of the British Red Cross Society which, in conjunction with the St. John Ambulance Brigade, has a really wonderful record of war service. Between D-Day and the middle of September nursing members put in more than 10,500 hours' duty. Calls for extra personnel came at all hours of the day and night when the wounded from France were passing through our hospitals, and no call was ever made in vain. ....the relatives of wounded who arrived in the town, tired, anxious, often distressed.... always found in the Red Cross and St. John members kindly, helpful and solicitous friends...*
>
> *"So too have the Women's Voluntary Services. Your mothers, wives, sisters and sweethearts who are in the organisation had three types of work to organise and carry out in connection with D-Day operations.*
>
> *"They supplied hot meals at all times to seamen who were voyaging to and from France continuously. These meals were cooked by the British Restaurants, which have become such a feature of our community feeding programme, and carried in containers to rest rooms or to the gangways of the ships in the Docks.*
>
> *"Then the W.V.S. supplied personnel to do domestic work in two emergency medical services hospitals. One of these workers was eighty-two years old, and she worked from midnight to 3 a.m. twice a week. Another useful service rendered by the W.V.S. was the supply of voluntary car drivers...*
>
> *"The Royal South Hants and Southampton Hospital and the Borough Hospital were chosen by the Ministry of Health as Port Hospitals for "port" casualties, that is cases which could not be sent further inland by train without further attention. The opening of the Second Front meant restriction on the use of the beds in both Hospitals, and only gravely ill cases were admitted. The R.S.H. received 1,786 cases after D-Day and the Borough some 900 cases."* **(Mayor Dyas in Southampton Forces Newsletter, July 1945)**

The eventual success of Operation Overlord brought changes to life in the town. There were no air raids after D-Day, although on 12th and 15th July 1944 respectively, there were attacks by solitary flying bombs, which caused much damage but no loss of life. First-aid posts and other civil defence facilities were closed in November 1944. Fireguard duties were reduced. On 31st October new street lights were being installed. Blackout restrictions were eventually eased. The evacuation scheme ended before Christmas 1944: 1,000 secondary school children returned to the town and the secondary schools, closed since 1939, were gradually re-opened.

MONDAY 18th SEPTEMBER 1944 *"...Some of the houses in the Drive had light curtains in their windows after dark, as allowed by law in some places. There is much confusion as to the position in Southampton. Some say that the "dim out" is allowed but I have seen nothing official."* **(Cox)**

SUNDAY 31st DECEMBER 1944 *"Frosty again all day, with a slight thaw in the sun. But the frost has now been in shady places for a week. There was some cloud first thing this morning but later it cleared and the sun shone all day. Evening clear and moonlit and frosty. A light cold wind. Went to work this morning. T.B. and George Donald ere the only two in, so there was not a lot of work done. All three of us finished at four o'clock. Mr and Mrs Rogers came up to dinner and when I arrived home this afternoon they were sitting in front of the fire yarning to mother about old times and old people. I washed and changed and soon after five we had tea, which was rather elaborate. Spent the evening reading and soon after nine the old people left. Elsie and I walked with them to the bus stop at the "Merry Oak". When we got back we had supper and then sat and listened to the Radio programme until the chimes of Big Ben announced that a new year had started. As usual the same note of optimism was prevalent in the New Year greetings and it seems fairly evident that the possibilities of peace are far greater than at any time since the war started. But how long yet before it all ends, I know not. The experts say, by the summer."* **(Cox)**

"The Red Cross Do-nut girls." American Red Cross women on the dock-side with the Queen Mary behind. (Newfield)

On 30th August 1939, the Queen Mary left Southampton for New York and did not return again for six years. She was converted into a troop carrier in 1940. In May 1942, the ship left New York on the first of the runs to Gourock on the Clyde, bringing American troops to Britain. These "Shuttles" started in earnest in June 1943, in preparation for D-Day. The ship could carry over 15,000 troops. On 11th August 1945, she was used with other liners to repatriate American and Canadian troops and take British war brides to their new homes.

American Red Cross refreshment trolley in a docks shed. (Newfield)

American soldiers in the docks. (Newfield)

American troops "Getting ready to go back home". (Newfield)

A 14th Port latrine. (Newfield)

High-ranking American officers. (Newfield)

An American kitchen, after the war. (Newfield)

Lt. Col. Meyer, Lt. Comm. Moses, Col. Kiser and an unknown American, say "Goodbye" at the railway station after the war. (Newfield)

Hotchkiss Machine-gun on Catchcold Tower, manned by the Royal Navy (H.M.S."Safeguard"), 23rd February 1945. (City Heritage Collections)

South side of the Bargate. (Note the Military Police sign.) The Bargate was used as an air raid shelter. (Southampton City Heritage)

American service personnel outside the Bargate. (Newfield)

American army officers, outside the Bargate. (Newfield)

Captain Dalton Newfield at the Bargate. (Newfield)

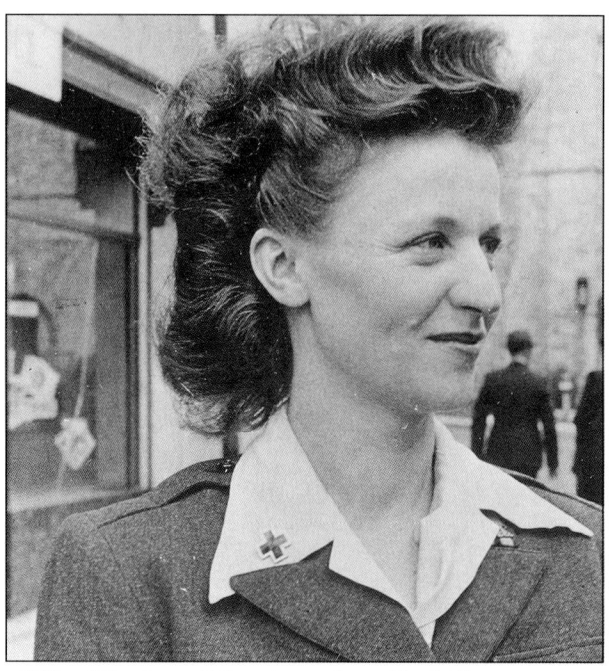

"Dals Boys". (Newfield)

Miss Rhodes of the American Red Cross, near the Bargate. (Newfield)

AMERICAN AND BRITISH TROOPS ABOUT TOWN

The American 14th Major Port were based in Southampton for over three years, from July 1943 until November 1946. Their presence, and the large numbers of Americans and Canadians passing through the town made a considerable impression on the local population and changed the lives of many. In February 1945, American soldiers started to use the town as a leave centre.

Problems between the Americans and the British had been anticipated by the respective governments and troop education schemes were set up in both Britain and America. British Welcome Clubs were set up to promote joint social events.

"The citizens of Southampton received the Americans with open arms." **(Knowles)**

"American and British troops worked amicably side by side in the cookhouse, on sanitary duties, and in the stores, the officers attaining a very high degree of interchangeability. Cordial relations between the two armies were rapidly established, and although in the earlier stages it naturally fell to the British staff to carry out, or at least direct, the majority of the work, the American staff was always seeking to help with the burden in every possible way." **(Brigadier Hanney, quoted in Knowles)**

American soldiers were supplied with rations to take when they visited local families. Many local people found themselves working with the Americans. The Americans organised dances and parties to which local women and children were invited.

There were problems however, recorded in the 14th Port Books written in early 1945. Many incidents of violence between service personnel in the town in 1944 are recorded in these books. Amongst the Americans themselves, there were 27 recorded cases of violence between black and white soldiers. There were 31 recorded cases of fighting between American and British personnel. The latter problem was first noticed in August 1943.

A memorandum dated 4th August 1943 from Rear Admiral J.M. Ripon at Naval Offices, Southampton:-

"To be read by all Commanding Officers of Ship to the whole of their assembled ships companies.

1. It has come to my knowledge that some ratings have been publicly abusing America and the Americans in this port, and in such a way that the Americans themselves were obviously intended to hear the words and expressions used.

2. I cannot sufficiently strongly condemn such behaviour.

3. Apart from the injury such conduct must do to the United Nations War Effort, it is disgusting that sea men of another nation who are, to so speak, our guests should be subject to such treatment. Even the wild Arab will not harm by word or deed a stranger who is visiting his tent.

4. No one that I have met has anything but praise and gratitude for the way in which our men have been treated on the other side.

5. I feel sure that it is only a small minority who I know would condemn such conduct to see that there is no recurrence of this blackguardly behaviour.

6. Anyone apprehended as taking part in such demonstrations will be dealt with most severely."

(14th Port Books)

In a letter dated 12th April 1944, an official of the 14th Port wrote:

"...there occurred last week eleven incidents of assault of U.S. Troops by members of British Armed Forces. Two of these incidents were by personnel of the Navy. Of the other nine incidents knives were used by the British Army assailants in three cases.

In each case the assailants have attacked individual Americans, and the method of approach in all cases is very similar. The American is either asked for a cigarette or for matches, then all his proffered cigarettes or matches are divided and he is asked if he is going to do anything about it. He is then invariably assaulted, and in three cases the victim has been badly lacerated by a knife. U.S. Forces are forbidden to take weapons of any form out of camp or barracks, and are searched before leaving. It is feared that unless these unwarranted and premeditated assaults are checked the U.S. Forces will secrete weapons outside their camp etc. and recover them on going into the town, and organize retaliation which can only result in serious bloodshed.

I consider it advisable that an order be issued forbidding all British Troops from carrying knives of any description when not on duty. This will bring the British Army into line with the present U.S. Army order which, I understand, is universal throughout England." **(14th Port Books)**

Reasons for the fighting were said to be the preference of many British women for American troops, the apparently greater wealth of the Americans and the consumption by the Americans of beer and spirits in short supply. Before and after D-Day, many local public houses ran out of beer.

"After diligently weighing all of these assaults, it is my opinion that the only motive is the resentful attitude towards the American soldiers by the British soldiers and sailors. Most of these incidents happen after blackout, and none of the subjects that were attacked could say that they could identify any of the perpetrators, except that they were sure of the soldiers and sailors they described as British." **(14th Port Books)**

To help curb the violence, British soldiers were prevented from carrying knives outside barracks. American and British Military Police patrols were stepped up. There were some more serious cases. By January 1945, one American had been court martialled for murder and one for manslaughter.

Venereal Disease

VD, a problem throughout the war, was causing local concern in early 1944. The local branch of the Women's Cooperative Guild petitioned the Borough Council for the notification and treatment of VD to be made compulsory, however the government thought this would lead to concealment.

The 14th Port troops were given educational talks. VD clinics were set up in all billets by the American Red Cross.

The 1945 annual medical report for the borough gives an indication of the extent of the problem for the local population. In March 1943, new clinics had been set up in the Old and New Docks for the use of British service personnel, in addition to the older clinics. The number of male patients attending the clinics with acute Gonorrhoea and Syphilis fell over the war period, partly due to new treatments for the former diseases. The number of women patients for both diseases rose markedly however, over the same period. In 1938, there were 334 male cases compared to 178 in 1945. For women, the figures for 1938 and 1945 were 64 and 170 cases respectively. "A distressing feature has been the numbers of young persons, especially girls, attending the clinics... ." There had been a steady increase in cases in the under 15, and 15 to 20 age groups.

"It was found that "Camp Followers" (prostitutes) were engaged in a lucrative business in this district following D-Day ...These girls, it was reported, were not local talent but usually came from London." **(14th Port Books)**

There were reports of prostitutes setting up business in buses on pay days. Others rented rooms, apartments and houses.

American Club Hoists Stars and Stripes

Flag raising at the recently opened American Red Cross Club in Southampton was marked by a ceremony in which representatives of the American and Canadian Armies took part.

The United States flag was hoisted by Miss May Coughlin, Assistant Director of the club, to the accompaniment of cheers from the soldiers.

Before the ceremony there was a softball match in the Park between a Canadian team and a United States team. The former won by seven to nil. Afterwards the players who were escorted to the club by the band of a Canadian unit, were entertained to tea and dinner.
(9th September 1943, Echo)

Vacation Courses for Visitors
Introduction to English Life

Designed to give members of the Canadian and United States Forces in this country some appreciation of English life, two vacation courses are being held in Southampton by University College in co-operation with the British Council and the Canadian Legion Education Service.

Thirty-eight Canadians - soldiers, sailors, airmen, fire-fighters, nurses and women of the Auxiliary Services - are attending the first course, which began on Thursday, and will continue until next Wednesday. A larger number of Americans and Canadians will attend the second course, which will follow immediately after the first.

A comprehensive programme, identical for each course, has been arranged. It consists of lectures, addresses and visits to places of historic or cultural interest. **(11th December 1943, Echo)**

The main American Red Cross Club was in the High Street, near the Bargate - in the building where Burton's shop now is.

An American Red Cross Club in Southampton, May 1945. (ABP)

Spirituals at Guildhall"
Coloured Choir Has 1,700 Audience

The United States Army coloured choir sang a programme of Negro spirituals to an audience of about 1,700 at the Guildhall on Sunday afternoon. The concert was given under the auspices of the Southampton Christian Laymen's Council.

The choir, which sang unaccompanied under the conductorship of its own chaplain (The Rev. James J. Smith), was welcomed by the Mayor of Southampton, (Councillor R. J. Stranger, M.C.) and thanked at the end of the concert by the Sheriff (Councillor J.C. Dyas).

Chaplain Smith conducted prayers and in a short address explained the meaning of the spirituals sung by the choir...
(13th December 1943, Echo)

Americans' Dance

Christmas Day ended at the American Red Cross Club, High Street, Southampton, with a grand dance attended by about 200 American Servicemen with members of the ATS, WRNS and civilians as guests. The Witch Hoppers dance band played, and a feature of the evening was a "jitter-bug" demonstration by "Tony and Mavis", of the Court Royal Hotel followed by a "jitter-bug" contest in which eight couples took part.

Turkey and plum pudding were served at dinner on Christmas Day and for tea the chef produced a magnificent iced cake - which was cut by the club director. **(28th December 1943, Echo)**

"Sgt Hyman singing, Lt. Busse dancing with Lt. Flanagan" (Lt. Flanagan is the woman). The band is the 14th Port Orchestra. (Newfield)

At a Polygon Hotel dance: "...Lovely Saturday nights". (Newfield)

"There were loads of troops in the town, mostly Americans; about 8 men to every woman so you can well imagine what a wonderful time I and all the other Wrens had when we went dancing at the Town Hall! We didn't take a bit of notice of the Doodle-Bugs going over the top. We had better things to do!" **(Jean Rouse)**

"When the Americans came there were a lot of soldiers around the town and they used to flock into the dances. ... There was usually a queue round the Guildhall before we opened and we would send an attendant out when we got about 900 in, to count down the queue. 1,000 was the limit." **(Harold Jackson-Seed, Guildhall Manager in the war)**

American Hosts
Southampton Children Their Guests

Three hundred Southampton children were the guests of the members of the American Army, Navy and Merchant Marine at a grand Christmas party at the American Red Cross Club, High Street, Southampton.

A 12 ft high Christmas tree, gaily decorated with coloured lights and lengths of coloured popcorn stood in the corner of the room in which the party was held. The entertainment consisted of conjuring by Professor W.H. Woodley, ventriloquism by Petty Officer A.G. Spicer, singing and dancing by Edna McCrindle, and community singing led by Mr. Judd.

The highlight of the afternoon was the arrival of Father Christmas (impersonated by Corporal Adam Szukalewicz) from a specially-built fireplace. He presented each child with a packet of candy, a packet of cookies, and fruit, all given by the Americans from their rations, and a toy.

(21st December 1943, Echo)

"We got on all right with the Americans, there wasn't much trouble. In fact we were all brothers in distress as it were, and even if they had made a bit of a late start, they were in with us at that time, and of course they made a tremendous difference both with their armed forces and of course with their material supplies. Most of them were much the same as any other servicemen, they were nice people who had been taken away from their homes!

...They had a plentiful supply of cigarettes of course and they were generous with them, as indeed they were with some of their field rations. In the days of the rationing I must admit we were very pleased to receive them!" (**Jimmy Mead**)

"Thornycrofts particularly used to get the bigger ships and you used to see a lot of American sailors and of course other nations as well, French, Belgian, Polish - oh yes quite a mixture of nationalities.

They got on quite well with the local people, of course some of the younger ones went away with the young ladies of the area, there used to be a lot of talk about that, the older people used to look down on that type of thing especially with the Americans - they had a bad name!" (**Bramwell Taylor**)

"...I mean outside our back gate there was a tent where they used to check vehicles and things coming through and initially it was a Tyneside Division who got pretty roughed up I believe at the actual landings, ...and then the Americans moved in and of course all the cigarettes and the sweets you know, and all the girls used to come up from the town and keep on pestering them for sweets. I think they got a lot more than they asked for from what we noticed on the barb wire afterwards." (**John Hobbs**)

"They wanted scotch you see and all, they always went for scotch and...I know one night we only had, because we were rationed with scotch you see...we only had this one bottle up, I remember...we put it up and suddenly the door opened and about six big Americans, two big coloured fellows among them, came in, and I said "Oh my goodness they're gonna drink all our scotch", so I thought "Well I'll have to put it away", because some of our regulars never got a look in you see, so I put it away and ...they all wanted scotch so I said "I'm sorry, a beer?"...they just had one beer and went, they went all round the town to find scotch.

...There was never any trouble with them they were always friendly...been more trouble with Scotsmen than the Americans...when they had a few drinks they used to get really funny." (**Ruth Bigwood**)

An American soldier and his girlfriend: "he married". (Newfield)

Above Bar in the mid 1940s. (Newfield)

Lt. Busse and his girlfriend Lt. Grace Waite (they later married). (Newfield)

A Concert at the South Western Hotel, December 1944. (ABP)

Lt. Grace Waite. (Newfield)

The "Forces" Rendezvous

The Guildhall was opened to Servicemen and women every Sunday night for the "Forces' Rendezvous".

*"The Rendezvous started in January last year when the town began to fill with Servicemen and women during the build-up for D-Day. It was organised by, and is still carried on by, the Southampton Christian Laymen's Council, who believe in providing for the whole man - comfort and refreshments for the body; and a simple, informal and undenominational service for the soul. Everything offered is enjoyed and appreciated. Quite often the address at the service is given by a Serviceman. Just before D-Day there was a party for 1,800, and there were even more than that at the Watchnight Service. In January the B.B.C. were back again with their microphones and recorded twenty five minutes' community hymn singing. You may have heard us in the Forces' Programme on Feb.4th." (**Mayor Dyas, Southampton Forces Newsletter, July 1945**)*

At a fete towards the end of the war (the month is June, but the year is uncertain). (Newfield)

71

NAAFI Club & Allied Welcome Club

In July 1944, a NAAFI club was opened in the old King Edward VI School in Havelock Road, the war damaged premises having been repaired.

"You've probably heard about our NAAFI Club. It's established in what was once the King Edward VI School, opposite the Civic Centre, and has now been running for about a year. It's something super in clubs. A chirpy little Cockney told me the other day that he's afraid to go in in case he sinks and gets smothered in the pile of the carpets! Well, perhaps they've never been in better equipped or more comfortable a club - and there's a warm welcome waiting for you there when you come home on leave, or, better still, for good. Just nearby, on the corner of Commercial Road and Cumberland Place there's an Allied Welcome Club. There are canteens and hostels all over the town and while I can't list them all I must mention that the one in the Avenue Congregational Hall has been open every night of the week during the whole of the war."
(Southampton Forces Newsletter, July 1945)

Coloured Troops Tour Town

Southampton "Citizens of Tomorrow", in co-operation with Chaplain D.A. Carty, arranged a tour of Southampton for a party of coloured American troops. The party was accompanied by members of the C.O.T. who joined them at lunch at the American Red Cross Club.

At police headquarters the visitors were greeted by the Chief Constable (Mr. P.T. Tarry, OBE), who gave a talk on the work of the police. Officers then conducted the party over police headquarters and the Law Courts. Councillor Mrs. R.M. Stonehouse showed the party over the Civic Centre and Guildhall. After tea the visitors viewed the Bargate, the Old Walls, St. Michael's Church and other parts of old Southampton. The rest of the evening was spent at Ashby Youth Club, Shirley.

As a souvenir of the tour the "Citizens of Tomorrow" signed a handbook of Southampton which was presented to Chaplain Carty by the chairman, Mr. John T. Stonehouse.

(6th June 1944, Echo)

York Gate, in the North Walls, Southampton (since demolished). (Newfield)

Local women with American sailors in a Southampton park.

"We all worked in a clothes shop in College Place and this photo was taken one evening in the parks with two American sailors." **(Joan Lamb)**

"One thing that stands out particularly was, after the pubs had closed you used to get hundreds, literally hundreds of...American sailors...coming back to join their vessels...and on one occasion...one of our chaps...thought he saw...a strand of hair poking out the...peak cap of one of these...sailors...he said "Just a minute...take your hat off". It was a girl, her locks fell out. She was taken into custody then...and it transpired that she was a prostitute. She'd made a terrific living out of associating with the Yanks." **(Phillip Longland)**

. "I knew a bloke down the Spring, who ran the Spring, and the Yanks came in. They didn't hang about, they had their bottle of whisky paid for and away...and went up their billet hall. There was a lot of that went on...but you forgave them because...well, what could you do, couldn't do nothing to stop it, even if you reported it you had no proof."**(Albert Hatch)**

"Oh yes, yes Americans had an image I mean I think the biggest thing were the uniforms, they were like silk. Just wonderful silk gaberdeen whereas our soldiers had really rough and badly made (uniforms)."**(Pamela Humphrey)**

"An American sailor with the ridiculous name of Everett Englebart, (he came from Ohio, of Norwegian descent), from one of the L.S.T.s, would always make a bee-line for Eddy (her sister) . Every evening they sat together hand-in-hand, on the wall, having fallen in love with each other. One evening when his ship was due to sail, he refused to leave her. His ship-mates desperately tried to get him away but in the end had to leave without him. A couple of hours later two S.P.s (Shore Patrol), at least seven feet tall, with their white belts and white gaiters glistening against their dark-blue uniforms, came and quietly spoke to him. They led him away sobbing. Meanwhile, the mothers watching this little episode, shouted out to him, "Go quietly son." Really he had no choice. Eddy never saw him again. His ship sailed, presumably never to return. Yet theirs was not the only love story with a sad ending." **Marion Ainsworth**

Sight-seeing at the end of the war. Lt. Busse and the Civic Centre. (Newfield)

American Sport

In October 1944, the 14th Port began to organise sports events for the troops. An American football team was set up, composed of players from all detachments of the Port. Practice grounds were obtained and The Dell used for matches.

"On 22nd October 1944, American football had its debut in Southampton before a combination of 5,000 GI's and curious civilians when the 14th Port Team, dubbed the "Pirates", dropped a 12-0 decision to the UK champion 8th Air Force "Warriors". From that first game and through the remainder of 1944, the "Pirates" played nine other contests to round out its season." **(14th Port Books)**

Later, a shortage of equipment and travel restrictions limited the sports programme to Southampton and the 14th Port area.

Basketball teams were formed in all port detachments - 12 teams in all. They took part in a basketball league, playing in Taunton's school gymnasium. Soccer, boxing and darts teams were set up. In January 1945 a Port Ping Pong Championship was held.

Major Bardella and the 14th Port flag, at the Dell. (Newfield)

American football at the Dell: "Dal and I and the gang! went each time". (Newfield)

WAR BRIDES

Many local women married American and Canadian servicemen and emigrated after the war.

Eleanor Clauson was the daughter of Leonard Charles Clauson, who worked for the Union Castle shipping line in Southampton. The family had lived in the Southampton area since Eleanor was one year old. They lived in Velmore Road, Chandlers Ford. Eleanor went to the Southampton Girls Grammar School. During the war, she served in the ATS at the HQ Chester Western Command, where she met American Captain Dalton Newfield on his third day in Britain. He was to become the Provost Marshal of the 14th Port in Southampton. Later Eleanor worked alongside the Americans in Winchester. She married Dalton Newfield in California on 22nd June 1947.

Eleanor Clauson. (Newfield)

"Well my Aunt Theresa, she met my Uncle Jim at Blighmont Barracks because they used to hold dances there, they were stationed in Millbrook, the Americans, and they used to hold dances and she went one night and met him and she fell in love straight away and she brought him home to meet us and it was very exciting really because they used to sort of come and visit us and bring, you know, tinned food like Spam and fruit salad and salmon that we didn't know about during the war and make a fuss of us kids, you know, with loads of chocolate and gum and, you know, as the jeep used to come up to our street all the other kids were quite envious as they came into our house and it was very exciting, he was a lovely person and of course, you know, they decided to marry before he left for D-Day and it was quite a rushed affair...

Ah yes, she married and we had a lovely wedding and I was bridesmaid and of course that was very difficult to arrange a wedding, you see, because the material was short for dresses and things like that so my mother did that for my auntie, she begged, borrowed and stole to get this wedding together. She had a lovely wedding in St. Monica's Church in Shirley and of course the Americans got her all the food she wanted. I mean, there was no shortage.

....in fact, in the street just a few yards from us two sisters married Americans. Their father was a baker you know." **(Pamela Humphrey)**

The Wedding of Teresa Bulford of Freemantle, and US Staff Sergeant James Dailey, 25th May 1944. Pamela Humprey nee Bowles is the bridesmaid on the left.

SOURCES

The Photographs:

Associated British Ports (City Heritage Services).

Dalton Newfield Archive (City Heritage Services).

Masterton archive (City Heritage Services).

Imperial War Museum.

Southern Daily Echo (Echo).

Royal Corps of Transport (RCT) Museum.

British Newspaper (BN) Pool (now defunct).

National Archives of Canada.

Cox Collection (City Heritage Services).

Private collections of Oral History interviewees.

Other Sources:

The diaries of Daniel Cox (Cox Collection, City Heritage Services).

The diaries of Gertrude White, nee Spring (Private Collection).

The 14th Port Books: "United States 14th Major Port, Southampton", 2 volumes, 1944-45 (City Heritage Services).

Regal Cinema (later The Odeon): Weekly Return Books (City Heritage Services).

Southampton Docks Handbook, 1947 (Special Collections, Reference Library).

"Memories of Southampton 1948 (American Souvenir Edition)" (Special Collections, Reference Library).

St. Johns School Logs (St. Johns First School).

Southern Daily (formerly Evening) Echo.

Archives in the Southampton Record Office (SRO), in particular:

"Annual Report on the Health of the County Borough and the Port of Southampton for the Year 1945", HC Maurice Williams OBE, County Borough of Southampton (SRO SC/H 1/66a).

Southampton Forces Newsletter, July 1945 (SRO D/Z 811/1).

SRO D/Z 428

SRO D/Z 472

SRO SC/TC File 194/9

SRO SC/TC File 194/13

SRO SC/TC File 195/21

Book Sources and Further Reading:

Hartcup, G: "Code Name Mulberry. The Planning, Building and Operation of the Normandy Harbours", David and Charles, London, 1977.

Hutchings, DF: "RMS Queen Mary, 50 years of Splendour", Kingfisher Railway Productions, Southampton, 1986.

Knowles, B: "Southampton, The English Gateway", Hutchison & Co. LTD., London, 1951.

Moberley, R: "D Day", in Hampshire Magazine Vol.9, No.8, 1969.

Willmott, WP: "June 1944", Blandford Press, Poole, 1984.

Oral History Interviewees:	**Addresses:**
Marion Ainsworth	City Heritage Collection Management Centre, Melbourne Street, Southampton, SO14 5FB.
Bert Bagg	
Frank Barrett	
Ruth Bigwood	Southampton Record Office, Civic Centre, Southampton, SO14 7LP.
Patricia Cameron	
Dorothy Harmsworth	
Albert Hatch	Special Collections, Reference Library, Central Library, Civic Centre, Southampton, SO14 7LP.
Violet Hoare	
John Hobbs	
Pamela Humphrey	Cope Collection, Special Collections, University of Southampton.
Michael Hunt	
Harold Jackson-Seed	
Joan Lamb	Southern Daily Echo, Above Bar, Southampton.
Phillip Longland	
Jimmy Mead	Department of Photographs, Imperial War Museum, All Saints Hospital, Austral Street, London SE11 4SL.
Jean Rouse (letter)	
Bramwell Taylor	
Wally Walton	
Kate White	Royal Corps of Transport Museum, RHQ RCT Buller Barracks, Aldershot, Hants., GU11 2BX.
	St. Johns First School, Castle Way, Southampton.